Friendly Guides to Technology

Friendly Guides to Technology is designed to explore important and popular topics, tools and methods within the tech industry to help those with and without a technical backgrounds come together on a more equal playing field and bridge underlying knowledge gaps to ensure teams, regardless of background, can fully work together with confidence.

This series is for people with a variety of goals. Either those coming from a non-technical background who work closely with developers and engineers, those who want to transition into the industry but don't know where to start as well as people who are looking for a clear and friendly introduction to a particular topic.

The series focuses on all areas of the modern tech industry from development, product and design to management and operations. It aims to provide a better, more well-rounded, understanding of the eco-system as a whole and remove as many barriers-of-access to the industry, be it cultural or financial, to ensure everyone has the ability to successfully learn and pursue a career in technology, regardless if they want to become a developer or not.

More information about this series at `https://link.springer.com/bookseries/17128`

A Friendly Guide to Software Development

What You Should Know Without Being a Developer

Leticia Portella

Foreword by Angela Bassa

Apress®

A Friendly Guide to Software Development: What You Should Know Without Being a Developer

Leticia Portella
Dublin, Ireland

ISBN-13 (pbk): 978-1-4842-8968-6   ISBN-13 (electronic): 978-1-4842-8969-3
https://doi.org/10.1007/978-1-4842-8969-3

Managing Director, Apress Media LLC: Welmoed Spahr
Acquisitions Editor: James Robinson-Prior
Development Editor: James Markham
Coordinating Editor: Gryffin Winkler
Technical Reviewer: Marco Rougeth and Luciano Ramalho

Cover image designed by eStudioCalamar
Illustrations by Giovanna Bissacot

Distributed to the book trade worldwide by Springer Science+Business Media New York, 233 Spring Street, 6th Floor, New York, NY 10013. Phone 1-800-SPRINGER, fax (201) 348-4505, e-mail orders-ny@springer-sbm.com, or visit www.springeronline.com. Apress Media, LLC is a California LLC and the sole member (owner) is Springer Science + Business Media Finance Inc (SSBM Finance Inc). SSBM Finance Inc is a **Delaware** corporation.

For information on translations, please e-mail booktranslations@springernature.com; for reprint, paperback, or audio rights, please e-mail bookpermissions@springernature.com.

Apress titles may be purchased in bulk for academic, corporate, or promotional use. eBook versions and licenses are also available for most titles. For more information, reference our Print and eBook Bulk Sales web page at http://www.apress.com/bulk-sales.

Printed on acid-free paper

To my mom, who showed me what strength is.

Table of Contents

About the Author

Leticia Portella is a Brazilian software engineer working at Stripe. She started her development career after learning programming as a hobby.

She has a bachelor's and an M.Sc. in oceanography and worked for many years as a numerical modeling expert at a coastal engineering consulting firm, helping build and improve ports worldwide. During her master's, she started learning more and more about programming until she finally switched careers.

Being a self-taught developer, Leticia understands deeply how hard it is to grasp the technical concepts for people without a computer science background. Because of that, she has dedicated her spare time to teaching people and humanizing the struggles of developers.

She wrote about her studies and career developments on her blog (https://leportella.com), and since then she published over 130 posts in three languages (English, Portuguese, and Spanish).

In 2017, she cofounded the first podcast about data science in Brazil, Pizza de Dados (a joke with Pizza and the word "Data" in Portuguese). Pizza de Dados educates its listeners on technical concepts through a light conversation with top Brazilian researchers. The work on this podcast resulted in her achieving the highest award of the Brazilian Python community, the Dorneles Treméa/Jean Ferri Award, for members who keep alive the spirit of collaboration, entrepreneurship, and commitment to the community.

ABOUT THE AUTHOR

Since 2021, she has been a teacher on the LinkedIn Learning platform. Her courses have reached thousands of students. Several of them praised how the author made the content easy to understand yet highly impactful.

Ultimately, she realized that technical concepts should be taught more broadly in a lighter and more fun way. This book is the result of that love for teaching and sharing.

About the Technical Reviewer

Marco Rougeth is an enthusiast and advocate of open source development and a prominent contributor to the Python community in Brazil. He is the Technology Director of the Brazilian Python Association (2022–2023). He was awarded Fellow Membership by the Python Software Foundation in Q3 2020 due to all his efforts in the Python community, especially in Brazil. He is also a software engineer at Amazon Web Services in Dublin.

Acknowledgments

I would like to thank James Robinson-Prior for trusting that this was a book worth publishing.

A special thanks to my dear friend Luciano Ramalho, who was a mentor and a cheerleader in the long process of creating this.

I would like to thank every person that gave me part of their time, giving me feedback on early chapters and ideas: Andréia Miguens, Kelly Moriarty, Rafael Santos Menezes, Carine Gursky, Surekha Rao, Ana Cecília Vieira, Jessica Temporal, and Tiago da Silva.

A special thanks to all of my beautiful friends who supported me in this long journey.

To all the beautiful teachers and mentors I had throughout my life, thank you for the patience you had and the time you gave me.

To Marco, the love of my life, I couldn't have done this without you.

And finally to my mom and dad, who gave me wings and made me believe I could go wherever I wanted.

Foreword

During my first year at university, I took a class that was advertised as an introduction to computer science. The textbook we used was titled *An Introduction to...* something or other. Back then, I thought of myself as decently well versed in programming. I wrote my first lines of scary-to-me code around age 8 or 9 (something that ultimately printed my childhood equivalent of "Hello World!" to the monochromatic green screen monitor) and even took an Advanced Computer Science course in my public high school, thank you very much!

So it was more than a little shocking when I felt like a complete failure in that university class. Despite my seeming advantages, I only barely scraped by (and still probably only because the professor and teaching assistants took pity on me and virtually held my hand throughout the semester). That experience made me feel stupid and this feeling stayed with me; I opted to pursue a mathematics degree instead.

Years went by, then a decade. It was always clear that I was passionate and skilled around computers, but I was still scared (and too scarred) to pick up a book on my own and start over. After all, stupidity is being presented with the same information repeatedly and not incorporating it into planning and thinking, whereas ignorance is rather the state of not having ever encountered a particular thought or experience before. If one of the best schools in the world couldn't get me to understand the domain, did I really think I was going to just do it on my own?

Still, like the ocean to Moana... "code" called me. At first timidly and, over time, more boldly and confidently I explored the topic from different frames of reference. I ultimately did fix up my mental canoe and set proverbial sail once more.

You see, it turns out that I'm not stupid after all! I had merely been ignorant of the things I was ignorant about and also too arrogant to accept the possibility I might not know as much about computer science as I imagined I "should" have known by then. I had lost much of the liberating curiosity that comes from admitting that it's OK to struggle with aspects of a discipline, or with teaching approaches, or to even just have so much going on that you have to step back before you push through.

It's also amazing and exciting because none of us know anything when we're born, other than our instincts. Imagine the little ignorant and pluripotent brains, just hopping from possibility to possibility until constraints start appearing either because of observed and imposed social norms, new learned heuristics, or even just good ol' physics. It's from that very ignorance that sprouts the drive for knowledge.

Unfortunately, many of us lose the ability to be silly and creative—or worse, we figure out that we may not have the safety to take reasonable risks. Still, every day I see people being vulnerable and doing great things. It happens when we finally have the courage to go after our hunches and make progress and when we can reframe failure as a positive outcome because of the lessons we learn with each attempt. This is the book I wish I had had when I started over.

I met Leticia in 2019 when we sat down for a conversation about data science and my experience managing teams of data practitioners in different industries. It was so refreshing to meet kindred data souls with whom I had so much in common: Brazilian-born women forging our path as technologists. I'm often awed by how, despite there being almost eight billion of us, we are so many things at once that we always have something we've shared with other humans.

Leticia's book shows you how software developers develop software without assuming your goal is also to develop software. We're witnessing rapid maturity in the craft of software development, and with the near inevitability of impacting others through and being impacted by software, it's only logical to be interested in learning how it all works. This book never assumes we're dumb if we don't find a concept intuitive, it assumes that we might just be ignorant—gloriously and verdantly ignorant!

This book is a starter kit to the immense craft of software development. Leticia lays out with clarity and purpose each of the many dependent, independent, and competing processes that make up successful software applications. If you want to better understand how the many software-driven automations that exist all around us are built, this book will shine a light on it all, without arrogance. I'm so grateful readers now have access to this insight, laid out with such wit and warmth.

—Angela Bassa,
Senior Director of Data Science and Analytics at iRobot

Preface

Who This Book Is For

This book was written for people that don't have a background in computer science and have little or no experience with software development.

It doesn't assume or expect that its readers will become developers, but rather gives a minimum technical context for those who want to work in the software industry and want to learn more about it.

It focuses especially on people that are working closely with a team of software developers but usually have a hard time understanding the context where they are inserted and feel like they need to learn the world to be able to work properly. These could be managers with a nontechnical background, product and project managers, designers, or even people establishing a new startup.

This book can also be interesting to people that are coming from more traditional companies to tech-focused companies, where the development is either the heart of the company or even the product itself.

Finally, if you are just learning how to code and would like to better understand the world you might end up working with, this book might help to give an overall view, but it is in no way a thorough guide. Extra materials are available in the "Further Reading" sections of each chapter.

Who This Book Is Not For

Throughout this book, I briefly introduce some concepts that are common in the industry, but the focus of this book will be on web applications, that is, software that can be used and accessed over the Internet.

If you have experience as a software developer, you might find this book very basic or even simplistic. The ideas here are not necessarily deep enough or detailed enough if you want to become an expert. There are also some concepts that are in some ways simplified because the extensive explanation wouldn't add value to the audience of this book.

How This Book Is Organized

This book is organized into five parts, following the experience of a person that is building a new ecommerce application.

Part 1 will guide you through the first steps of a software project. It also starts with some introduction to technical concepts assuming no previous knowledge from the reader.

Part 2 provides a deep dive on the technical aspects of a web application, from the overview of how communication happens on the Internet to how web applications typically work. This is the most technical section of the book.

Part 3 will focus on the more practical aspects of building software products like the critical decisions that need to be made and methodologies to actually build the product.

Part 4 goes over the aspects that can guarantee a software project to be successful in the long run. It gives a clear idea of why there are so many things that one needs to do to guarantee good projects and that most of them aren't visible to the user's eyes.

Finally, Part 5 talks about the people that build software, how teams work, and the different roles that are involved and takes a deeper dive on the role of developers in all of this.

Conventions

<u>Underlined</u> text identifies a new word that is available on the glossary.

Text in monospace font identifies something technical or a piece of code.

Boxes emphasize a concept that was just introduced.

PART I

Getting to Know This Familiar Unknown World

CHAPTER 1

Welcome!

If you can't explain it simply, you don't understand it well enough.

—Unknown author

You probably woke up by an alarm set on your mobile phone, maybe learned about the weather on your smartwatch, or checked some emails on your computer. Words like apps, smartphones, smartwatches, and software are so common nowadays that sometimes it's hard to remember that most of these things became part of our daily lives not so long ago. I remember that was in my first year of college, back in 2008, when a friend showed me that his mobile phone could access the Internet. My first thought was "Why is this useful?". Silly me.

We interact with all these technologies every day, all day. Software is everywhere, and yet it is still growing its presence in more and more areas. It's close to impossible to live without it nowadays. Thus, it's natural to see that companies are investing in more technologies while the demand for technology-related roles is growing.[1]

Regardless of industry your company is now a software company, and pretending that it's not spells serious peril.

---

[1] "The Future of Jobs Report 2020" by World Economic Forum: `https://fdly.li/01-02`

—David Kirkpatrick in "Now Every Company Is A Software Company" in *Forbes*: `https://fdly.li/01-01`

Software is entering every part of our lives, and the reality is that your involvement with this world is an unescapable reality. You will, in one way or the other, interact with software and the software industry.

Even if you are not directly involved in the creation of it, some companies have software as the *core* product, meaning that even roles like sales or partnerships need to understand how these technological products work.

So we fall into a scenario where software is everywhere, and yet it still seems magical to so many people. This creates a segregation between people that know and understand this world and people that don't. That's a huge problem.

We can only build software for *everyone* if *everyone* is involved in the construction of software. Anything besides that is utterly flawed. The only way we can guarantee we have technology that *actually* changes the world is if we include everyone in the conversation. And if your life will more and more be guided by software products, why not be part of this change?

> We can only build software for *everyone* if *everyone* is involved in its construction.

The problem is that most content about the software industry are focused on developers. If you do not want to become one, what do you do? People are left to "learn on the job," needing to balance demanding roles while trying to learn an infinity of concepts. In a worst-case scenario, they can be paired with some insensitive people that can make things even more complicated. In another worst-case scenario, companies require everyone to have been a developer somewhere in their careers, just worsening the gap. As the software development is becoming the industry standard, that is the recipe for trouble. We must fix that.

I believe that one of the main sources of pain in the tech industry is precisely this poor communication between people that understand technical concepts and people that don't. The interaction is crucial for the success of projects and products. If we can make technical concepts broadly available and easily understandable, we will achieve better communication which will undoubtedly lead to better relationships, better work environment, and better software.

1.1 Why Am I Writing This Book?

I come from an untraditional background, teaching myself how to code and then learning most of the things about software development on the job (with help from a lot of very patient people). While coding seemed complicated at first, learning how to code was far less complicated than understanding how to actually develop software.

I had to rely on people to explain the concepts and processes I needed to do my job, and the result was not always the best. I know for a fact what it's like to have a *very* insensitive person looking down at me because I didn't know this or that concept. Frustration doesn't begin to explain. The feeling of being a fraud is always in the corner, waiting for the next unknown concept to surface.

In my path, I was lucky enough to have multiple excellent mentors to each bad one. People that kindly and patiently explained concepts that seem impenetrable at first. As I gained more and more experience, I realized that the reluctance of people to explain these concepts in a simple way is usually a symptom that they don't understand them well enough.

All this allowed me to relate with people that struggle with the technical jargon. As time went by, I tried more and more to help people understand about technology in many different places: from meetings to blog posts to courses and even on conversations at a pub. One of my favorite things is trying to explain to my mom and her friends about this world I live in, in a simple and accessible way. I find that most of the time their interest is suppressed by a feeling of "not being smart enough," not lack of curiosity.

> Anyone can learn about software, even if they don't ever want to become a developer.

My goal with this book is to teach technical concepts to *anyone* that is interested in learning them. I want to give a general understanding of what the software industry looks like, how we build software, and what are the main concerns while doing so. I want you to be able to talk to an engineer and understand why they might have trouble with some features or why they should spend more time building something that the user can't see.

I want to show you that understanding these technical concepts isn't "too hard" and that you, me, and anyone can learn them if we want to. Most of all, I want you to feel confident that all this world of technology and software is for you and that you can change it even if you never write a single line of code in your life.

1.2 How Will We Learn Together?

In this book, we will follow your journey while building a new software product from scratch. It starts with you joining a new company, Jolly Co, where you are asked to develop their new product: an ecommerce for customers to buy products directly from farms.

Typically, software is made of multiple cycles of development, also called iterations. We will follow one cycle, from development to delivery of a product. This iteration of development can be actually divided into smaller iterations of planning, executing, and delivery until the first version of the product (known as Minimum Viable Product, or MVP) is done.

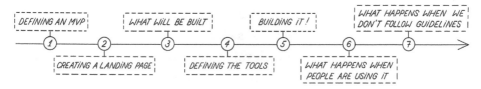

Figure 1-1. *Software development is made up of multiple cycles, and we will follow one of them from conception to execution and delivery. We will also take a quick look of the future*

We will start by defining who we are building it for and which kind of problems it will solve first by defining what will be built on the first version, MVP, of your product (Chapter 2).

Then we will want to tease our potential customers to what we are building. This is when we will learn the basics of websites and how to create a landing page, which is a page to allow customers to know that something is cooking in the oven (Chapter 3).

Once we have that, we need to start understanding a bit more what needs to be built (Chapter 4) and the tools we will need to do so (Chapters 5 and 6). While choosing these tools, there's a lot we must consider so we don't accidentally shoot ourselves in the foot, so we will spend some time discussing them (Chapter 7).

Finally, we will spend some time understanding how we can transform all these into something concrete by learning how to build software (Chapter 8) and what we should worry about while building it (Chapters 9 and 10).

Although most of this book will be focused on the construction of a new software product, we will also learn about what happens once the product is out of the door and we have people (typically called users) using it (Chapter 11).

We will also take a quick look at what would happen in the future if we decide not to follow the standard guidelines we discuss throughout this book (Chapter 12).

Once we understand product development, there is a whole part where we will discuss the humans that build software, which is a component that will be present in all phases of the development. We will discuss things that affect a team's ability to produce software (Chapter 13), how developers typically work (Chapter 14), and all the wonderful people that are part of this process (Chapter 15).

Shall we?

CHAPTER 2

The Birth of a Software Project

The future cannot be predicted, but futures can be invented.

—Dennis Gabor

Everything usually starts in the same way: there is something that can be solved or improved by the use of technology. Maybe it is an idea that someone had while seeing themselves or their friends struggle with something. Maybe a user that reported some extra functionality (usually called <u>feature</u>) they need. Having an idea for a software can be, by itself, something really hard, but having an idea doesn't really get you anywhere. You still need to figure out what to do from there.

Let's imagine that you started a new job at Jolly Co, a new tech startup that is helping manage farms' inventory. Now they are thinking about a new idea: selling from farms directly to end customers. This is a different market for them. Until now, they have been selling to farms, so they are what is called a <u>Business to Business (B2B)</u> company, and this new idea would open a new market on the <u>Business to Consumer (B2C)</u> area.

This new product, called JollyFarm, will be made from scratch. You just joined the company and are responsible to make sure this project is a successful one. Taking a product idea and transforming it to a list of what

© Leticia Portella 2023
L. Portella, *A Friendly Guide to Software Development*,
https://doi.org/10.1007/978-1-4842-8969-3_2

needs to be built (also called <u>requirements</u>) is one of the first steps, and its value can't be underestimated. But how can we make sure we know exactly what to build?

2.1 Understanding the Hypothesis

The first step is trying to really understand the problem you have in your hand. In this case, the problem is

---

Food reaching the customers isn't as fresh as they would like.

Then, you come up with an idea for a product that could solve this problem. In our case, the idea is to create an ecommerce that will sell food directly from the farm to the customers.

This idea might be great, and you might feel super excited to roll off your sleeves and start working! However, you should consider that this is just a hypothesis and only a hypothesis.

Hypothesis   Customers will prefer to buy the food directly from the farm to get fresher products.

You might be wondering: Why is this a hypothesis? Although ideas might sound great, there's a difference between an idea that *feels* great and an idea that will actually become a viable product. Treating the idea as a hypothesis allows you to try to validate it: Will users use it? Like it? Pay for it?

2.2 Validating the Hypothesis

A good start is to look at potential competitors. Can you find other companies doing the same? How do they target their product? Do they have good reviews? As important as the question "what are they doing well?" is the question "what are they missing?".

Are there competitors? What are they doing well? What are they missing?

The good news is that having competition doesn't mean the idea is useless. Sometimes, just being *better* is enough. In fact, you can actually say that having competition is actually a *good* thing as you can showcase that there is a potential market for the product. Now you start asking yourself:

What would make this product better than the competition?

Making a product better is not only a matter of shiny new features. It can mean a lot of different things like making it more economically viable, giving a better user experience, etc. For instance, Amazon changed the entire industry of ecommerce not by selling new products but by providing a completely different experience on delivery of products.

There is only one way to figure out what would make users want a product, and the answer is quite simple: talk to them.

Failing in meeting customer expectations is a big problem in the software industry. In the past, some companies would spend months, even years, building products without talking to a single customer. After tons of money and time spent, the product would be in the market, and guess what? Nobody wanted it.

In today's world, a company that doesn't try to understand their customers and their problems won't survive. Most big companies will have at least one of their values associated with "customer obsession" or something similar.

Customers are the only people that can truly tell what they want and what they need. So your first task is to go out and find some potential users. Ask some of them to meet you and listen to them!

Talk to potential users. Get data!

One question that you might be thinking is "how many users should I talk to?". The answer is not so satisfying: it depends. Sometimes, one or two users with good perception and lots of experience are more valuable than a hundred users. Start with a couple of users, gather your ideas, and see what you discover. If you feel like new interviews are not getting anything new, you probably already have more than enough!

2.3 Preparing for a User Interview

Before talking to potential users, it's important to define what you want to get out of the interviews: Do you want to get their pain points? Try to see if they would be a good fit for your solution. The goal will depend on which stage your product is on: idea phase, prototype phase, development phase, or launch.

In your case, you need to know their habits of buying organic food to get a better understanding of how the JollyFarm can help them with that. You know this won't be easy to get out of them, so you have to be prepared with good questions that will lead toward a good direction. Here are some of the things you must consider:

Formulate good questions

A good question is formed as a setup (what/why/how/when/where) followed by the question you actually want to answer. For instance:

"When you are buying food, how do you decide which brands to buy?"

Beware of leading questions

You always want to avoid leading your users toward a specific direction. Instead of saying something as "How often do you go to The Happy Peach supermarket?", you could say "How often do you buy vegetables?". Leading questions are more useful if you suspect that the answer will be the opposite of what you lead the user to think about.

Another use of leading question is to build confidence and trust at the beginning of an interview. Some users will be uncomfortable or shy at these interviews. You could use some leading questions to get them to a comfortable position and use the more complex questions for when they are feeling better in the situation.

Don't ask questions with yes or no answers

When you have a meeting with a potential user, you want to make the most of it. You need them to expose the most that they are willing to. Questions that have a short yes or no answer are not good questions for them to elaborate answers. Make sure you allow answers that can get them to share more of their experience.

Be aware of bias

We all have bias, and it can be presented as conscious and unconscious bias. When you are testing your hypothesis, you might be willing to guide them toward the answer you want to hear. One way of avoiding any personal bias is to hire someone to make the user interview for you. As not everyone can afford to do that, think of your questions and everything you talked in an interview. Avoid phrases like "I know I always...," "I prefer...," and so on. This is not the moment for you to share what you think is right, but make sure you are covering all corners.

Don't ask what they want

You should use this time to understand their environment and problems, but you shouldn't ask users what they want. In most cases, what a user says they want is not necessarily what they need. As the famous phrase associated[1] with Henry Ford says:

> *If I had asked people what they wanted, they would have said faster horses.*

While doing user research, you should always be careful to look for the hidden needs of users. Make sure your questions try to expose their needs rather than desires.

A question that can get you a lot of insight is: "If you had a magic wand and could change one thing about your experience, what would it be and why?". This question can lead to very surprising answers! The users will have a free space to talk about any of their pain points, and you didn't lead them anywhere.

Make it interesting

Every time you talk to a potential user, remember that this person is giving you some of their time to help you build something better, so try to make it as fluid and interesting as you possibly can. Questions should be built on top of each other, to make it personal enough but still get all the answers you need.

Keep notes!

Keep track of everything that users came up with, even if they don't sound important at first. It's always useful to come back to these notes later in the product development process. Maybe something you dismissed at first can be highly valuable later on! If you can't keep up with listening and making notes, bring a second person. This is valuable information!

---

[1] Although you find the association between this phrase and Henry Ford, there is no clear evidence that he ever said it. The first appearance in books is from 2002. Source: https://fdly.li/02-01

2.4 Creating JollyFarm User's Questions

As you can see, there is a lot to think about when doing user interviews. You decide to ask just five questions[2] as the basis of your interview and decide to leave the rest of the interview to be adapted to the user's answers to these questions.

1. **What's the hardest part about buying fresh and organic food?** The idea behind this question is to understand the main pain points. What are the problems they are spending the most time on? It helps you confirm that the problem they have is the problem you are working on.

2. **Tell me about the last time you encountered this problem?** This helps them give the context in which they are finding the problems.

3. **Why was this hard?** This question helps you to understand more about the problem but also how you can market the product later.

4. **What, if anything, have you done to try to solve the problem?** It can give you a better idea if their problem is big enough for them to try to solve it and what the competition looks like.

5. **What don't you love about the solutions you've tried?** It gives you ideas on what can make your product different and better!

---

[2] As suggested by Eric Migicovsky in the talk "How to talk to users": https://fdly.li/02-02

Having a small number of questions is good to focus the interviews, especially when the person you're talking to doesn't have too much time. However, if they are engaged and have the time, make sure to use their questions to deep dive on the topics!

Regardless of the questions you are asking, there is one golden rule here: this is the moment to listen, not to talk. Don't try to convince them your idea is great. Don't try to sell them your product. This is the moment to get precious insights on how you can make your product a hit!

Avoid doing the talk. User interviews are listening time!

2.5 Allow Yourself to Change Directions

Now you did the hard work. You found users, talked to them, and understood their needs. You have tons of notes and are trying to go through them all. What do you think about it? How do you feel about your idea? Do the answers you got show your hypothesis is a bit closer to the truth? Or do they show you they are completely different from what you expected?

Check the answers you got with your idea. Are they still aligned?

After all this work, if you don't think you are solving the right problem, maybe it is time to rethink things. Maybe you even left the meetings with a different idea that will make you start over. Although this might sound a bit frustrating, this is an amazing result nevertheless: you avoided building the wrong product from the start! Imagine how much time and money you might have spent to only later discover it was not the thing people wanted.

When a company changes their business idea based on new market trends, it is said that they <u>pivoted</u> the idea. Several big companies have done so. For instance, Starbucks started as a company to sell espresso machines.

If, on the other hand, you are still excited and see some potential, great! You maybe even left this process with more ideas that when you started the process. No matter what the result is, you've learned something, and it is extremely valuable because we are in the beginning of the whole process.

2.6 Defining Your Target

OK! So you talked to a couple of users and validated your idea, and Jolly Co decided to move on with the project. Now it's time to define who you are building this product for.

Initially, you can think that *anybody* can be your target market, but that's too broad. It's much easier to define and work for a specific target audience than it is to make a large audience happy. If you don't, every person in your project might have a different idea of who "the user" is or even think that your users think and act the same way they do. Narrowing down your target users allows you to move faster, deliver better software, and make you spend less money.

A good way to structure your company's goals and target market is to fill out this sentence:

(Product) is a *(general, relatable tool)* that allows *(2 adjectives + target users)* to *(use case)*.

For the JollyFarm, this is the goal and target market:

The *JollyFarm* is an *online ecommerce shop* that allows *modern families with small children and working parents between 30 and 40 years old* to *purchase healthy and fresh food directly from local farms.*

Now you know exactly who you will target. It could be that down the line, a couple of months from now, you will find out that seniors that are worried about their health are using your app. It doesn't matter! Defining a target user will make it easier to guide the development of your product, especially during the initial phases when you have so much uncertainty.

This pitch is good for giving a broad definition of the company and target market, but it's still too broad for helping guide the development of your software. Even if you think that "modern families with small children and working parents" seems to be small enough of a target, it's not. Users aren't all alike, they have different goals and act in different ways.

2.7 Narrowing Down the Users

One alternative to deal with this undefined, abstract set of users is to create what is called personas. A persona is a realistic character sketch representing one segment of a targeted audience. The idea is to create realistic and tangible personalities that could be used to bring life to the discussions involving a user.

You can think of it as if you are creating characters on a movie: they need a name, a background story, and a personality. The more details and realistic descriptions, the more believable they are. You can mix personality traits and characteristics of multiple users you interviewed to bring them to life.

Figure 2-1 is an example of Maria, one of the personas created for the JollyFarm.

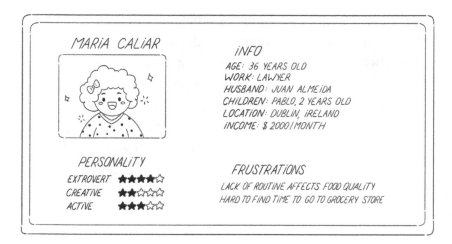

Figure 2-1. *Example of a persona for the JollyFarm*

Once you define personas, you can start using them to guide your development. Each persona, because of their unique goals, attitudes, and behaviors, will take a different journey through the product.

This will allow you and your team to focus on solving their problems, without being drowned in the large quantity of uncertainty that you have in the beginning of the project. They also build empathy. You might say "this won't work for Maria, because she doesn't have the time." You are building for someone, not for an abstract idea of someone.

2.8 Define What Should Be Built First

As we get closer and closer to the goals in your project, you might be tempted to think about *all* the features your users may want. In reality, most users won't use most features, and the most likely scenario is that a couple features will solve the problem of the majority of users, at least in the short term. It's usually referred to as the 80/20 rule,[3] where it is expected that 80% of users will only use 20% of the features.

If we know that most users will only use the most basic features, why will you spend time and money in all features before ever delivering the most needed? What if we just build the 20%? Or maybe not even 20% but enough to check if a large set of users like the product and buy it?

This is the concept of building a Minimum Viable Product (MVP). The MVP is a small project, with few features (yet very important ones), that will be used to validate your product idea. Because it's small, it can be quickly done, the development of it won't cost as much, and you can iterate on it as you get the user's feedback.

An MVP can be as simple as an online form to receive orders. It doesn't have to be deeply technical, as long as it reaches its goal: testing the hypothesis and checking your assumptions.

Imagine your user gets back to you and say "I want a sailboat." What do you think when they ask you that? What plans come to your head? How long will it take to deliver a sailboat to this user of yours? Take some time thinking about this.

If you think a little bit beyond what they said, you can see that what the user actually wants is not a sailboat. They want a faster way of moving from point A to point B through water. However, they don't really want to wait for you to spend two years to build a boat. And you can't really build parts of a boat, right? What will your user do with just paddles or a sail?

Since you know what they want—move faster—you can still start small, but not with a paddle. You can give them a small canoe, then add paddles, then the sail, then a motor, making it faster and faster but always useful. With this mentality, your user has the ability to move from point A to point B at all times, even if they don't have what they initially wanted. They

---

[3] This is called the Pareto principle and the correct phrasing is: "for many events, roughly 80% of the effects come from 20% of the causes."

didn't have to keep walking for two years until you gave them a sailboat. The MVP is not a single paddle, it's a canoe: something that will get them moving even if it is not exactly what they want.

Figure 2-2. *The ideal MVP will allow users to use the product from day 1, even if it is not the ideal solution for them*

For the JollyFarm, we defined that the MVP shall be

Users will be able to see products and make orders.

2.9 Understanding Software Requirements

At this point, your idea starts to become more concrete. You have a good understanding of the problem and users. It's time to think about building this product: Is the MVP definition enough?

Imagine for a moment that you're in the kitchen and decide to cook dinner. You turn to your roommate and ask them what they want to eat. They can say something generic like "beef" or give you a recipe for beef bourguignon. Those are two very distinct answers, right?

Requirements is a pretty common term in the software industry, and you'll see it everywhere. The big problem is that, similar to the recipe answer, it can vary from a high-level, abstract statement ("beef") to a very formal and descriptive definition of a part of a system (beef bourguignon recipe). The different definitions will depend on the person you are talking to: a software developer, a manager, a product manager, or the user. High-level requirements are often called *user requirements*, while technical or detailed requirements are called *system requirements*.

What happens is that requirements can easily become a problem because they can have such diverse meanings. If you tell someone you want "beef," you can't really expect that they cook something specific, right? That's why you must understand who you are communicating with and align with them what type of requirements they need and expect. What we have for our MVP definition is a high-level requirement at best. To build something, we need to have more concrete system requirements.

2.10 Requirements Are Tricky!

Imagine for a second that your product is ready and you received a requirement for a feature from a business executive of your company:

The system should generate a monthly report of the products bought by each user.

What do you expect this system to do? Well… a report, of course! But think about it: Is this a *user* requirement or a *system* requirement?

Let's think about this report a bit more. What else could we consider while developing this feature? You decide to go back to the person that defined that requirement and discovered a couple of additional information:

- The system shall generate the report after 17:30 on the last working day of the month.

- The report must contain each user and product, the quantity, and the delivery fee.

- Report will be sent to the administrators via email.

Wait a minute! This is quite a different picture! There is a lot to think about when looking at this second list. Let's detail what kind of work this second list unveils:

- **The system shall generate the report after 17:30 on the last working day of the month**: This means that we need to have an automated task that will be executed every last working day of the month to gather these results. The system might not be prepared to execute automated tasks, so this is an additional work.

- **The report must contain each user and product, the quantity, and the delivery fee**: You need to know the order quantities per customer, which means that we need to be able to identify each customer. What if we don't keep customer information and everyone buys products as a guest? This means we need to include something like an authentication system so we can identify them. A user will need to be able to sign up, log in, change their password, and so on. This can be, per se, its own huge feature that may have its own requirements. If this is a new feature in an old software that doesn't have an authentication system, this may take a long time and deeply influence the development of the report feature. And we have more decisions: if you didn't have past customer information... what shall the report be like?

- **Report will be sent to the administrators via email**: There
  must be a system that will be triggered to send emails
  every time the report is ready. You also need to identify who
  the "administrators" here are. Maybe there isn't a way to
  differentiate common users from administrator users.

As you can see, there was a lot that was hidden under the first high-level description! In fact, even this second level of requirements can still unfold many more requirements.

Does this mean the first requirement is useless? Of course not! That type of user requirement is great to explain the feature to someone that wants to know more about the project, like an investor. However, when talking to the people who will start to implement the project, maybe even the second requirement list might be too high level.

Multiple times I've seen teams not being clear on what "requirements" actually mean. This leads to hidden features appearing when they are least expected and most unwelcomed. Before talking to stakeholders or developers about requirements, you need to make sure everyone is aligned on expectations. Don't allow room for surprises along the way!

An average of 34% of projects have a scope creep and an average of 12% fail completely, but the numbers can be even higher, depending on the maturity of a company.[4] When extra features are hidden under high-level requirements, they will impact the overall scope of the projects and undoubtedly affect deadlines.

Of course, it's impossible to know everything in advance and have every single detailed requirement before you start your project. However, the alignment of expectations will avoid many known pitfalls and can go a long way in helping avoid frustrations and scope creep down the line.

---

[4] Data from the 2021 report *Pulse of the Profession* from the Project Management Institute: https://fdly.li/02-03

2.11 Defining Requirements of the JollyFarm Ecommerce

Now that we spent some time with potential users, we need to sit down and define a list of requirements we need for our MVP. To do that, we need to remember a couple of things:

- **Avoid implied requirements**: If it isn't described, it shouldn't be in the product. As the report feature we just talked about, if only the high-level description is given, you shouldn't think that the developers will guess that you need an authorization system!

- **Avoid ambiguity**: You shouldn't use vague or subjective words. If you say something like "the system must support multiple currencies," it may open to interpretations of what "support" means: Is it to display? Accept payments in multiple currencies? Those can be two *very* distinct things!

- **Make sure you log your decisions**: Things change and sometimes you just can't remember why you went through a path! Make sure you keep the decisions that changed the requirements and who were involved in those decisions.

Let's consider again our MVP definition:

Users will be able to see products and make orders.

You know that a lot can be hidden here. Take a look at what we have: Is there something we need to unpack further? What do we actually mean by this definition?

You actually want a website where a user can see the products. This means that farmers must have the ability to add their products and the price of each one as per different units they sell it (kg, gram, unit, etc.). They also need to be able to add the amount they have in stock, and if a product doesn't have stock, it shouldn't be listed. They also need to be able to add new products that were produced, and each product that was bought should be removed from the stock.

The MVP definition, when drilled down, has actually two areas of work: one where the farmer can handle the products and stock and a second one where users can see and select products. As you think more and more, this single requirement actually becomes this list:

- A farmer's area where they can

  - Create a new product. The product should have

    * Name

    * Production/Collection date

    * Quantity in stock

    * Size

    * Photos

    * Unit sold

    * Price

    * Expiration date

  - Add stock to an existing product

  - Remove stock when a product is bought

  - Delete a product

  - Edit information regarding a product

- A user area where they can

  – See a product listing page. Features required:

    * List products that are in stock

    * List products without stock as "unavailable"

  – Check each product detail page. Features required:

    * See photo of the product

    * Show information of the product

  – Add items to a cart. Features required:

    * Add a product to a cart

    * Edit a product in the cart

    * Remove a product from the cart

    * Confirm a purchase. This should contain

      - A contact phone

      - An email

      - A valid delivery address

    * Remove items from stock once the purchase was confirmed

Imagine that you have all the preceding features. If you allow for users to make orders over the phone and pay in cash when the farmer is making the delivery, you already have a whole product. All the other features are important, but if we think of the 80/20 rule, we can drill this list down to

- Farmers can log in to the system.

- Farmers can see a list of the products they have.

- Farmers can create a new product.

- Farmers can update information from an existing product.

- Any person can see a list of products available from all farms.

This way, you are minimizing implementation and have a set of requirements to start with. Congratulations! You have started your project!

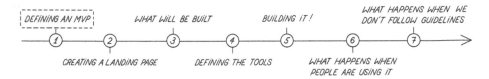

Figure 2-3. *We just defined what goes into the MVP, time to take a look at what it takes to create a landing page*

2.12 Chapter Summary

In this chapter, you've learned a lot about the foundations of software projects. User feedback is the center of any modern business product. User interviews are a great way of getting feedback and making sure you are going toward the right product and the right direction, and they can be useful in all phases of the project: from early days to working product.

Once you validated ideas with users, it is time to define what is the minimum product you can build that will solve a user's problem. This is usually referred to as the MVP, and it's based on the Paretto rule that roughly 80% of your users will only use 20% of your features.

Finally, you need to specify requirements to start building the product. Those can be very high level (called user requirements) or very detailed and technical (called system requirements). Because the meaning of "requirements" can change from person to person, it's important to always align which kind of requirements everyone is expecting.

2.13 Further Reading

This chapter is a high-level view of the work of a UX designer. I used the book *UX Research* from Brad Nunnally and David Farkas as the basis for a lot of this chapter: `https://fdly.li/02-04`.

I highly recommend the talk "How to talk to users" given by Eric Migicovsky on the Y Combinator: `https://fdly.li/02-05`.

I like the practical examples of building personas of the book *User Is Always Right, The: A Practical Guide to Creating and Using Personas for the Web* by Steve Mulder: `https://fdly.li/02-06`.

The book *Sprint Design* by Jake Knapp explains the methodology of creating and validating a hypothesis in a single week: `https://fdly.li/02-07`. I highly recommend the printed version so you can easily find the checklists the authors add to it.

The *The Mom Test* book by Rob Fitzpatrick was really amazing, teaching about how to talk to users even if they are not being super honest: `http://fdly.li/02-08`.

The book *Lean Inception: How to Align People and Build the Right Product* by Paulo Caroli is a great practical guide to use the Lean philosophy in product building: `https://fdly.li/02-09`. We will talk more about Lean in Chapter 8.

Finally, the book *The Nature of Software Development* by Ron Jeffries is a really lighthearted book that is one of the sources of inspiration to this book. I highly recommend reading it: `https://fdly.li/the-nature`.

CHAPTER 3

You Are Surrounded by This World!

Any sufficiently advanced technology is indistinguishable from magic.

—Arthur C. Clarke

Right now, we have a clear idea of our potential users' needs. You understand their pain points, and we have a good idea of how we might solve them. The next step is being able to translate these ideas (and requirements) into a software system. And to do that, we need to first take a step back in understanding what kind of systems are there.

Before we continue, you should know that this chapter assumes no previous knowledge of anything that's software related. This means that we will go over some topics that may seem too basic to some. I just want to make sure everyone is on the same page before we move to deep waters in the next chapter!

3.1 Two Sides of the Same Coin

Nowadays, most electronic devices—smartphones, smartwatches, televisions, computers—are complex machines. However, they can be roughly divided into two parts: a physical part and a virtual, more abstract,

L. Portella, *A Friendly Guide to Software Development*,
https://doi.org/10.1007/978-1-4842-8969-3_3

part. Anything that you can touch (all the cables, keyboard, mouse, etc.) receives the generic name of hardware. When you interact with these hardware using a program, you are interacting with software.

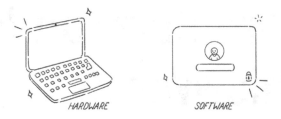

Figure 3-1. *Most electronic devices can be divided into two parts: a physical part called hardware and a virtual part called software*

If you have trouble remembering, there is an old joke that helps me remind which one is which:

Hardware is the one you kick, software is the one you curse.

Hardware and software are two sides of the same coin. Without the latter, the only thing you can do with a hardware is display it. Without hardware, there is nowhere you can use a software.

One of the most fundamental software that exists is the one that can interact with the hardware, called operating system (OS). The OS is dedicated to making the middle ground between you and the hardware. In fact, any hardware that you can think of has an operating system: from your smartwatch to cars and even elevators!

Windows is the most popular OS for personal computers and laptops, followed by macOS.[1] Smartphones also have operating systems, such as iOS and Android.

---

[1] Numbers from the Wikipedia page, `https://fdly.li/03-01`, accessed in January 2022.

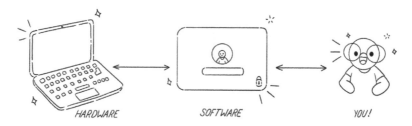

Figure 3-2. *An operating system is a software that allows people to interact with hardware*

An operating system isn't only special because it can communicate with the hardware. They also have another superpower: they allow other types of software to be executed (or <u>to run</u>) on top of it.

When you turn your computer or smartphone on, you are seeing the OS turning on. If you move your mouse around, searching for a specific program, or searching for a file, you are interacting with the OS. However, when you open a photo, the OS starts a different software, one specific for displaying photos. The same happens when you try to open a video or a text file. All these specific types of software are called <u>application software</u>. It's easier to recognize these applications in mobile smartphones, as we are used to installing and deleting them, but they exist in all OS out there.

While the OS focuses on using the hardware resources, the application software focuses on the interaction with the user. They run seemingly on the OS, so close that you probably missed the difference between them.

That's why, when we talk about software, we can think of it as a series of layers: one built on top of the other. The fun part is that you can interact with (and build) all of them!

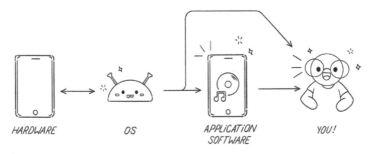

Figure 3-3. *Application software are the programs you usually interact with, like your text editor or video player. It's a type of software that runs on top of an operating system, and you, as a user, can interact with both!*

When we use application software in computers or laptops, we usually call them *programs* or *desktop applications*. In smartphones and tablets, they are called *mobile applications*, but usually referred to as *Apps*.

3.2 Accessing the Internet

The same way you need a specific software for playing a video or listening to music, you will also need one to access the Internet; these are called web browsers.[2] Mozilla Firefox, Google Chrome, Internet Explorer, Safari, and Edge are all browsers that are available in many OSs.

When you open a browser, usually the first thing you do is type something on an area at the top of the screen, called the *navigation bar*. Let's say, you type Wikipedia's main page: *wikipedia.org*. This thing you typed is called a URL (Uniform Resource Locator) or *web address*. Once you hit Enter on your keyboard, you will see that something is rendered in the lower part of Figure 3-4. What is rendered is called a web page.

---

[2] In practical terms, the Internet and the Web are different things, but for the sake of simplification, they are used interchangeably in this book.

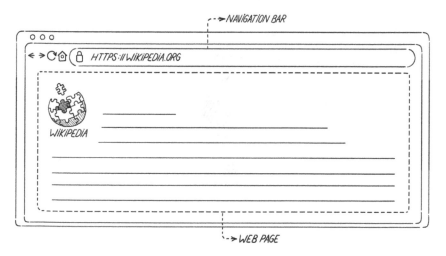

Figure 3-4. *The navigation bar of a browser with a URL is used to access a web page displayed inside in the bottom part of the screen*

The rendered web page looks nice, with images, colored texts, etc. However, the web page itself is just a file with instructions that tell the browser how to present some information. It's the browser's responsibility to interpret these instructions and render the web page accordingly.[3]

---

[3] We will discuss more about how a browser can get the file and render it in Chapter 4.

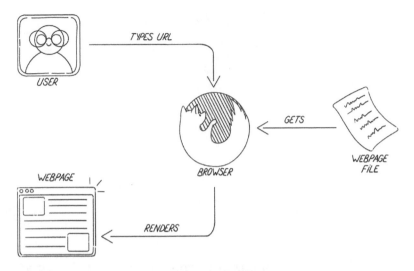

Figure 3-5. *When you type a URL into a browser, it will search for that web page file and render it to you based on the instructions contained in that file*

A web page is usually grouped together with other web pages under a similar context, forming a group. A group of web pages is called a <u>website</u>.

Figure 3-6. *A web page is a document with instructions of how it should be rendered by a browser. Here, you can see two web pages that are part of the website* wikipedia.org

3.2.1 The Logic Behind Web Addresses

In Figure 3-6, the right page has wikipedia.org/wiki/muffin. Why is that? How was this defined?

For a URL to be valid, it needs at least two parts separated by a period. The first part is called a <u>domain</u>, and in both cases earlier, the domain is wikipedia. The second part is called a <u>top-level domain,</u> and in the past, this was used to characterize which type of website this was, but this is long gone today. The most common top-level domain is .com, but there are more than 1500 options available.[4] Those are the minimum information you need for a new URL of a website.

---

[4] As of 2021: https://fdly.li/03-02

In reality, they are so intrinsically coupled that you usually just say *domain* instead of each part. Whenever we want to have a new website, we need a domain to associate the website with. In our case, we bought `jollyfarm.co` and will use it to make our website accessible!

However, as you have learned already, websites can have multiple web pages. Each web page must have one unique address to reach it. Because of that, each web page needs a unique URL, so we need tools to be able to create them.

One way to create unique URLs is to use a *subdomain*. A subdomain is an optional part of a URL that comes before the domain. In Wikipedia, the subdomain is used to redirect the website to a specific language.

Figure 3-7. *A URL consists of two required parts: the domain and the top-level domain. Optional parts, such as the subdomain, can also be included*

There is yet another optional part of the URL: the *path*. The path, similarly to the subdomain, allows us to create another unique URL for another web page in the website. In Wikipedia, paths are the way to get to a specific item of the encyclopedia.

Figure 3-8. *Paths and subdomains are used to create new unique URLs*

In a broader look, there isn't any[5] difference between a path and a subdomain; they are just ways to create unique URLs. Since one website can have many (*many*) web pages, you need one unique URL per web page, and that's why we have so many options.

The Wikipedia using subdomains for language and paths for each item was a choice made by Wikipedia's developers. They could have done it in very different ways, such as defining the language as part of the path, like /en/wiki/Muffin.

...

Although one URL can only ever lead to a single web page, you could have multiple different URLs leading to a single web page. Everything is a matter of choice by whomever is building the website and its URLs.

Figure 3-9. *Each URL can lead to a single web page, but different URLs can lead to the same web page*

So far, you've seen a lot about browsers, web pages, and URLs, but how do all of these things relate to software?

---

[5] Paths are case sensitive, while subdomains typically aren't.

3.3 Where Does Software Exist on the Internet?

We've seen that an application software can run on your computer or your smartphone, but what about the Internet? Every website you open is a type of application software. They can be simple (like a blog) or complex (like a social network or a banking system), but they are all applications. We usually refer to them as *web applications*, and that's exactly what JollyFarm ecommerce should be—and the main focus of this book.

Desktop applications   An application software that runs on computers.

Mobile applications   An application software that runs on mobile devices, such as smartphones and tablets. Usually just called an App.

Web applications   An application software like Gmail or Facebook that runs in servers (we'll see more about this later) but can be accessed by a browser, like Chrome. In contrast with desktop applications, web applications always require an active Internet connection.

Web applications can be accessed via different software. In a computer, the most common way to access them is via a browser. However, other products can also access the Internet, such as an App that allows you to receive and send emails.

Let's take a look at some web applications that you use every day!

Search engines

There are over 1.9 billion websites all over the Internet;[6] you need to have a massive engine to catalog and find the information most relevant to you. Search engines are websites dedicated to search for information based on words (or numbers, images, or anything really) and find it among billions of websites. You probably use search engines multiple times a day, every day.

When you go to a search engine and look for a *blueberry muffin recipe*, you are not asking for a single thing. You are actually adding three *keywords* so the engine can look for content that has a relationship between these three keywords together, but not necessarily the exact words. That's why sometimes you can search for a couple of keywords, and the engine suggests other keywords that are usually coupled together.

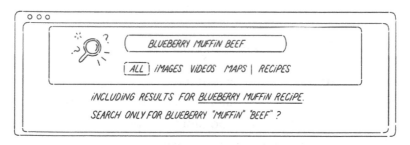

Figure 3-10. *The results for three keywords in a search engine. The engine will look at how the keywords relate to one another and which kind of documents relate to them the best*

Messaging apps

These are as common as search engines! Messaging apps are scattered over most of our social media platforms, and you can even use a chat to get support from some companies.

---

[6] Stats from `https://fdly.li/03-03` in Sep 2022.

One interesting characteristic of messaging apps is that in most traditional websites you make an action (click a link) and then you get a response (a new web page). Imagine if this was required for messaging apps: every time you want to know if there is a new message, you need to refresh the page. That would be horrible, right? In an online conversation, you want to receive a message even if you didn't click anything. Thus, messaging apps require a different type of technology. They are complex systems that you interact with multiple times a day.

Streaming services

Streaming services are a great example of complex software products that you interact often. Picture now that amazing new action movie being streamed in your TV with maximum resolution. How much information is flying to your TV per second? The software that run streaming services are very complex and need to be able to handle *a lot* of data going into your TV.

Users that bought this...

When you go to your favorite ecommerce and add a product to the shopping cart, you will soon see that there is an extra area on the web page saying "Users that bought this also bought these products," and then there is a list of products that would match nicely with the one you chose.

These are called recommendation systems, and they are a type of software based on data of users that are similar to one another. The idea is that similar users like similar things. So these systems try to use your previous behavior and the behavior of other users similar to you to try figuring out what you like.

3.4 Software and Programming

OK, so you know that JollyFarm needs a web application to connect farms and consumers, but how to make that become a reality? The way we build software applications is through programming.

Imagine you are in the kitchen on a glorious Sunday morning, and you decide to cook pancakes to make everyone happy. You go to your recipe book. Think about it: What is a recipe? It's nothing more than a set of instructions that should be followed in order, using the correct ingredients and instruments.

Contrary to what a lot of people think, computers can't think on their own (at least not yet!). They need sets of instructions to let them know what to do. They need to understand what should be done and when it should be done. These instructions are called <u>algorithms,</u> and they need to be precise; otherwise, computers can't perform correctly. While in a recipe you can say "add as much salt as you want," in an algorithm you can't leave room for interpretation.

Similarly, if a recipe is written in a language that you don't speak, you can't do anything with it. Computers also need their algorithms to be written in a way they understand, and the way to do it is by using <u>programming languages!</u> A programming language is just a *language* that allows people to write the set of instructions in a way the computer can understand. The name isn't in vain: programming languages are called languages because, similar to our <u>natural human languages</u>, they need to be written with a certain structure (syntax) and must have a meaning (semantics).

All the applications we've talked about until now, from the operating systems to recommendation systems, are written using one or more programming languages. When a programming language is used to write an algorithm, the resulting text is called a *source code*, or just <u>code</u>.

A code is the result of writing a set of instructions, that is, an algorithm, using a programming language.

When I was first learning how to code, I watched an amazing class[7] where the professor said something that I never forgot:

> *A computer will do what you tell it to do. That's very empowering. It's also very annoying. Because it means if your program doesn't work, it's your own darn fault. You got nobody else to blame but yourself. Because it's not the computer's fault. You may want to curse the computer, but you shouldn't. It's just doing what you told it to do.*
>
> —Prof. John Guttag

These defects that make some code not work properly are called <u>bugs</u>.[8] While you might be tempted to think that developers will spend most of their time writing new pieces of code, the reality is that the vast majority of time they will either be fixing bugs or changing existing code to have new functionalities (*features*).

3.5 When Code Is Working

Some algorithms are straightforward enough that they can be kept in a single file, usually called a <u>script</u>. On the other hand, complex applications require several files that are interconnected and likely don't work on their own. This collection of files containing code is called a <u>codebase</u>.

---

[7] MIT 6.00 Introduction to Computer Science and Programming: `https://fdly.li/03-04`

[8] Some people attribute the word *bug* to a defect due to an incident on the gigantic room-sized computer called Mark II, where a bug inside the machine caused problems. Although it is an interesting story, the word is reported as a synonym since the 1870s. Source: `https://fdly.li/03-05`

SOURCE CODE   SCRIPT   CODEBASE

Figure 3-11. *When an algorithm is written in a single file, it's typically called a script. A set of files that work together is called a codebase*

When the code can be *executed* by a computer, the result of a working codebase is called a <u>program</u>.

Whenever we say *software*, we are in essence talking about a program—a piece of working code executed by a computer—but also about other things, both tangible and intangible. Software also englobe data, documentation, rules, and procedures that go beyond the program that's running.

When people start to learn how to code, they likely start with small scripts that they can run manually every time they need. But learning how to build *software* demands one to learn more than just to write working code.

For the JollyFarm, we'll need a software that is complex and will become more complex over time. We need to consider multiple things before we start developing the MVP to make sure we are setting us up for success. We will learn more about the characteristics of programming languages in Chapter 7.

3.6 From the Developer's Computer to the User

Before starting to work on the MVP, we want people to start getting excited about what you are doing. What we can do is create a sort of "movie trailer" but for our product. We can now create a simple one-page website, just so people know what project is being built and with some contact information to reach out if they are interested. This website is called a landing page, and it's a good way to start getting visibility, even if you don't have a working product. One of the developers sat down and wrote the code for this website. What now? How can others access it?

When the code is still in the computer it was written in, we say it's in the development environment or devbox. At this stage, it isn't accessible to anyone beyond the developer who wrote it. To make sure that the code is available to anyone over the Internet, the software should go to the production environment. In production, as you can imagine, the system requires a lot more care and attention than what is required on the devbox.

The process of moving a piece of software from the development to the production environment is called a deploy (or rollout), and it's a critical part of the process because this is the moment where bugs can be introduced to a working system. If the devbox doesn't reflect the environment that exists in production, the process becomes even more critical, because you can never guarantee that the code will work seamlessly.

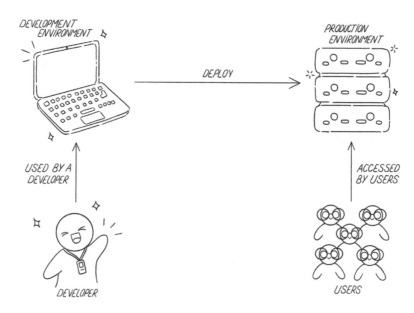

Figure 3-12.   *The development environment is where the developer can write code. The production environment is where the software is available to anyone to access it*

Now that the landing page was deployed, people can see that something's cooking in the oven. Nice! However, there's still a long way to go until we have a working web application for the JollyFarm ecommerce. We still need to understand a bit more about how they work once they are in production!

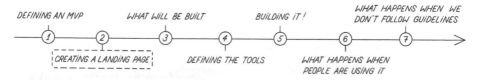

Figure 3-13.   *We now have a landing page, and it's time to start to understand what needs to be built*

3.7 Chapter Summary

Most electronic devices can be divided into a physical part, called hardware, and a virtual, abstract part called software. Software applications can be of three types:

- Desktop applications that run on computers.

- Mobile applications that run on smartphones or tablets. Typically called an App.

- Web applications that can be accessed via the Internet. The most common type of web applications are websites that can be accessed by browsers using web addresses, also known as a URL.

All software is written on computers using programming languages. When a programming language is used to write a sequence of logic steps, the result is either a script (single file) or a codebase (several files) that will be the basis for software.

When code is written in a computer, it's said that it's in a development environment and can't be accessed by anyone except the developer who wrote it. When it's broadly available to any user over the Internet, it's in a production environment. The process of moving from a development to a production environment is called a deploy.

3.8 Further Reading

Most of the materials used for this chapter came from the introduction to computer science classes or distilled technical content from computer science books.

One of my favorite go-to explanations on how computers work is the *Computer Science Crash Course* carried out by Carrie Anne Philbin on YouTube (`https://fdly.li/03-06`). It's a deep dive—to the point of explaining the electronic parts of a computer—but it has a dynamic and easy language.

The *MIT class 6.00 Introduction to Computer Science and Programming* teaches the basics of programming, but its focus is on teaching the basic of computer science knowledge, such as the basic of algorithms: `https://fdly.li/03-07`.

I already recommended it in Chapter 2, but the book *The Nature of Software Development* by Ron Jeffries is also a great source of reference and discusses as well some of the technical concepts: `https://fdly.li/02-08`.

PART II

Let's Get Technical!

CHAPTER 4

What Happens When You Open a Website?

"It's complicated."
"Yes, until someone explains it to you."

—Fredrik Backman

In the previous chapter, we launched our new ecommerce landing page, and now you want to show your family so they can see it. Your mom goes to a browser and types the URL you gave her: `jollyfarm.co`. Have you ever considered what happens when she presses enter?

We learned in Chapter 3 that when she types a URL, the browser will get the web page file and follow its instructions to render the web page. The file is stored in a computer—called a <u>server</u>—that can receive requests and return responses.

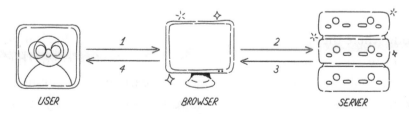

Figure 4-1. *When you type a URL, such as* `jollyfarm.co` *(1), the browser will go to a server that has the web page file and ask for it (2). The server will then return the file (3) that is rendered by the browser (4)*

© Leticia Portella 2023
L. Portella, *A Friendly Guide to Software Development*,
https://doi.org/10.1007/978-1-4842-8969-3_4

A server is a computer that can return data (like a file) when requested.

In the preceding example, you saw that a browser communicates with a server. However, browsers aren't the only applications that can access the Internet. Other applications, as mobile and TV applications, can also make requests to servers. That's why we generically call a <u>client</u> any application that can connect to a server. A browser is just the most common client you know, but there are many others.

A client is any application that can connect to a server. One server can receive requests from multiple clients.

Clients and servers are the fundamental concept of software systems. Web applications can improve on this concept and create more sophisticated versions of it, but they all have some version of this structure.

The question that comes now is: How can your mom's client know which server stores the file for the `jollyfarm.co` web page? There are thousands and thousands of servers storing million web pages; how can it know where to ask the file from?

4.1 Finding a Single Computer in the Web

The Jolly Co office exists somewhere in the world, and you want to tell everyone where they can find it. If you want to use a system that is unique in the entire world, you should use the latitude/longitude system. This system was built in a way that no two places on earth have the same location. However, it's unrealistic to go to your customer and say "You can find us at 27°36'03.9"S 48°26'58.3"W." It is much better to say, "We are located on Valley Avenue 32." Addresses are a way of simplifying location in a way that a human can easily understand.

The Internet works in a similar way. Each computer receives a unique IP address that identifies that particular computer in the network, the same way a latitude and longitude identify a unique place in the world. An IP address is a sequence of four numbers,[1] each varying from 0 to 255, separated by dots, such as 192.45.3.29.

Now imagine remembering the IP addresses of all your favorite websites. Madness. That's when the DNS enters the game. You can think of DNS as a gigantic phone book. They keep all the names of websites and their equivalent IP addresses.

Figure 4-2. *A DNS resolve will use the names of websites to get the IP address. This is similar to when you use a phone book to find your friend's number*

When you go to the browser and type jollyfarm.co, your browser first makes a request to a DNS resolver to get the IP address associated with that URL. Only then the browser makes a request to that IP address, reaching the server of the website you are trying to access.

---

[1] This format is the version 4 which is the most common. There are other versions that follow different formats.

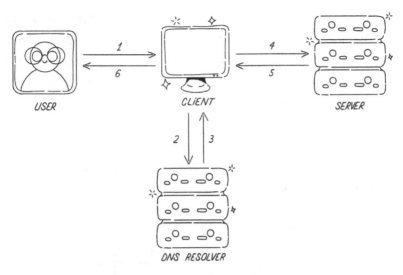

Figure 4-3. *When a user types a URL (1)—such as* `jollyfarm.co`*— their browser makes a request to the DNS resolver (2) that replies with the IP address of the computer where the website is stored (3). Then the browser will make a request to that computer (4) that will return a file as a response (5). The file will be rendered by the browser, and the user will see the website (6)*

Now we know how the client can find the server. So how can it actually request the data from it?

4.2 Communication over the Internet

Imagine for a second that you are living in the past when the only way you can communicate is via letters. You want to share some good news with your friend. How would you do it? A letter must have a structure, usually starting with something like *"Dear Lizzy, …"*, content being divided into paragraphs, and a proper ending like *"Love,"* and your name. In order to reach your friend, it should be placed in an envelope with an address. All these are communication *protocols*, a contract that both parts agree to abide. When everyone sticks to the protocol, communication can happen effectively.

Over the Internet is the same thing: *clients* and *servers* have a protocol for communication, called HTTP.[2] Similar to what would happen if you received a letter in a language that you don't speak, if a server is expecting an HTTP message but gets anything else, it simply doesn't know what to do with it!

Let's take a look on what kind of information can go in an HTTP request.

4.2.1 The Required Part

An HTTP message needs at least two things: what the user wants and the address of that message. The address will be the web address of that website, so in our case it will be `jollyfarm.co`. The *what* is sent through what's called an HTTP method.

The most common HTTP method is the GET[3] method. A GET method tells the server that the client is requesting the content for that page.

When you go to `jollyfarm.co`, what happens under the hood is that the client sends an HTTP message to the server. The HTTP message is sent with a GET method and the web address of the website.

We can see the whole process in Figure 4-4.

---

[2] Although being the most famous, there are many, many others. HTTP is the most common on typical web applications that we will address in this book. There is a specific way for emails (SMTP), for accessing files (FTP), watching a stream video (UDP), and many more.

[3] It is standard to write HTTP methods as upper case letters, to indicate the protocol method rather than a regular verb.

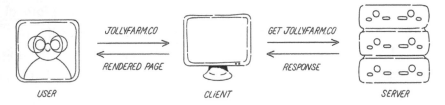

Figure 4-4. *When you ask for a web page, what happens is that the client sends an HTTP message with an address (*jollyfarm.co*) and the action to perform. In the case of just retrieving information, the action is represented by the HTTP method GET*

The method GET is the most common method, but there are others, each one focused on a particular task you want to do.

If you go back to Section 2.11, you'll see the requirements to deal with product inventory:

- Create a new product.

- Edit product information (like adding and removing stock).

- Delete a product.

- See products available.

This list of requirements represents all the four actions we can do when handling a piece of information: retrieving (product information), creating, updating (editing product attributes), and deleting.

All of these operations have equivalent HTTP methods that tell the server what to do with the information being sent, and those are the most common HTTP methods. These four basic operations are commonly known as CRUD (create, retrieve, update, and delete), and most systems will need to have some kind of CRUD to perform the basic tasks.

Operation	HTTP Method	Action
Retrieve	GET	Retrieve information that already exists
Create	POST	Send new information that will be added to the system
Update	PUT	Send information to update data that already exists in the system
Delete	DELETE	Delete an information that already exists in the system

CRUD are the four basic operations to deal with a resource information: create, retrieve, update, and delete.

Generic way to represent paths

In Figure 4-4, you can see the request is GET `jollyfarm.co`. If we wanted to get the page for products, we would make a request GET `jollyfarm.co/products`. These requests are being written with the address being a full URL (domain, top-level domain, and path). However, we can use a different representation to get the idea. We can use relative URLs.

To simplify things, we can represent the main domain (*jollyfarm.co*) as the symbol /. So we would have the following representation:

When we type…	We represent as…
jollyfarm.co	GET /
jollyfarm.co/products	GET /products

The symbol / represents the <u>root</u> part of a website, the first web page the user will see when they type the domain. Following the root, we have the paths to identify specific pages. This way, if for some reason the domain changes, all references will be working, because they are looking for the root of the web page, not for that URL in particular.

4.2.2 Where We Send Data

Whenever you need to send information from one part to the other, the information is added to another part of the <u>request</u> message, an optional part called <u>body</u>. When you fill in a form to create a new product, all the information of this new product will be inserted into the message's body along with the method and path.

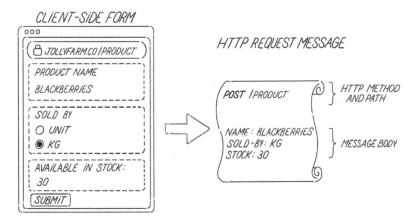

Figure 4-5. *When you fill in a form, all information added is inserted in the message's body*

How we organize data: the key-value pair

If you look carefully to the request in Figure 4-5, you will notice that the body uses a sequence value-colon-value. This is one of the most common ways of exchanging information, called a *key-value pair* structure.

A key-value pair is a way of structuring data in two parts separated by a symbol such as a colon. The first part explains what that data is about, and it's called a *key*. The second part is the information itself, and it is called *value*.

Take, for instance, the structure of the name of the product we've seen earlier. The *key* is called **Name**, the separator is the colon, and the *value* is the name **Blackberry**.

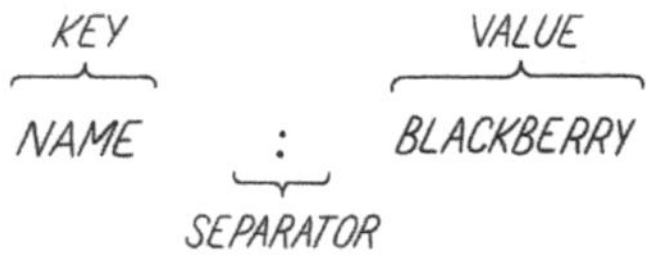

Figure 4-6. *A key-value pair structure consists of two parts separated by a separator symbol, such as the colon. The first part, called key, explains what the data is about, and the second part, called value, is the data itself*

The key-value pair is a very common way of storing data. So common you've used it already! A phone book is a type of key-value pair where the key is a person name and the value is the telephone number.

4.2.3 Information About Information!

So far, we know the request has

- The address of where in the server the request must go

- The body containing the information that is traveling from the client to the server

Are we missing anything?

Let's say that the information on the body was written in Japanese. The server might need to be aware of the language of the request in order to properly handle the characters as well as be able to return a response also in Japanese, right? But how can it know?

What we need is information about the information being passed through the request, which is called <u>metadata</u>. The body is reserved for information that the server should act on, and any information beyond that doesn't fit that purpose. The <u>headers</u> are a part of the HTTP message to keep the metadata of a message.

You can see that the request consists of three parts, and two of them are optional. When the client creates the message, it separates them by a blank line each. Only the first section is always required.

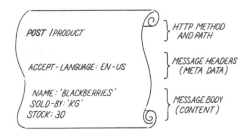

Figure 4-7. *A request consists of three parts: an HTTP method and a path form the required part. Then headers and body are optional parts of the message*

As you could see on the request, we can add a header that is called `Accept-Language`. This will let the server know that the message it will receive in the body can be interpreted in English. This information couldn't fit anywhere else in the request!

4.3 Protecting Your Data: Why the S in HTTPS Means So Much

If you pay attention to the websites, you will notice that most don't use HTTP, but rather HTTPS. The *S* stands for *secure*, which means that instead of using HTTP messages as we've seen earlier, it uses an additional process to make the communication more secure.

Consider that you are paying for a product and you type all the information of your credit card on a form. This information will also travel through the Internet to the server. What would happen if someone could break into the connection? They would have all the information they need to process any amount on your credit card! Not good at all.

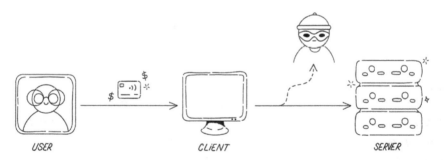

Figure 4-8. *There is a long way between the client and the server. Malicious people can get in between this connection and get access to all content being exchanged, such as credit card data*

The difference between the HTTP and HTTPS is an additional layer of security that guarantees that any information traveling from the client to the server is secured in a way that no one else can access it.

In an HTTPS connection, when you open the web page for the first time, the server will send something like an open lock to the client. When it's time to send data back to the server, the browser puts the data inside a "box" and locks it using the lock received previously. The client will then send the locked box back. The "box" can safely transit through the Internet back to the server. Because the data is locked with a lock that no one else has the key, there is no way that anyone can open the box and see the content.

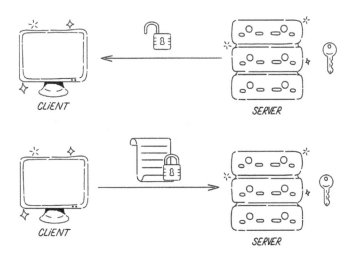

Figure 4-9. *In an HTTPS connection, the server sends an "open lock" (called public key). When sending data to the server, the client encrypts the data using the public key. Only the server has the private key to open the file, so any malicious person that gets the data in between the connection won't be able to access the data*

In reality, this process is infinitely more safe than a physical lock. The process is so secure that it is virtually impossible to break this lock. Even if someone manages to get access to the data between the client and the server, they can't see any of the data. That's why in the modern world, it is unlikely to find a trustworthy website that doesn't use HTTPS (and please don't put your information on one that doesn't!).

This whole process is called *encryption*, and this particular type of encryption is called a public-private key encryption. The lock is called a *public key* (because it can be broadly shared), and the key that stays in the server is called a *private key* (that can never be shared).

There is also a reverse process happening with the client sending an open lock to the server. When you access your bank website and want to see the list of transactions you've made, you also want this information to be secured, so the inverse process also needs to happen in the other direction.

When a website uses HTTPS, the browser usually shows the URL next to a padlock icon. If it doesn't, some browsers use it as an open padlock or a message such as *Not Secure*, as you can see in Figure 4-10.

Figure 4-10. *When a website uses HTTPS, the browsers usually display a padlock next to the website URL, while if they don't, it is usually displayed as an open padlock or a Not Secure message. Some browsers can add bigger and brighter messages for nonsecure websites*

4.4 Status Code: Discover What Happened with Three Numbers

You've learned how an HTTP message has at least a method and a path. This is only true for *request* messages, the HTTP messages going from a *client* to a *server*. The *response* message is a bit different, and one of the most important things that a response has is a status code.

A status code is a three-digit number that will allow the client to understand what happened to the request message that was sent. The most common status code is 200, which indicates a successful request reached the server and the response is what the client expected.

There are many, many status codes, and you don't have to know them all[4] as I am certain nobody does. Thankfully, they are divided into five categories, identified by the first digit of the response. By seeing just the first digit, you can have an overall idea of the problem:

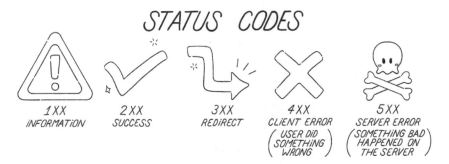

Figure 4-11.   *There are five categories of status code in an HTTP response: informational, success, redirect, client error, and server error*

Status codes that start with 1 are informational, which means that the server got the request and is returning some information back that is not necessarily what the client wanted. This means that the client might need to do something else.

When they start with 2, it means that the request was successful as the client expected.

A status code that starts with 3 means that the request was redirected to a new path. This could happen, for instance, when you have a new domain and don't want to lose requests that are going to an old one, so you redirect them to the new domain.

When starting with 4, it indicates that the client did something wrong: they are not authorized to access the server, they typed the wrong password, etc.

---

[4] If you are curious, have some laughs while learning status codes on `https://httpstatusdogs.com/`

Finally, a status code that starts with 5 means that the server did something unexpected. Typically, it means there's a serious problem in the server, and there's not much a client can do to fix it. An elevated number of 5 means that your system is in trouble!

One important thing you should know is that the status code returned by a server is defined by someone while developing it. This means that you can't be certain that the response will always have the most accurate status code. It isn't unusual to see status 200 (that usually means success) with a message like "request failed." This is definitely not a good pattern, but it happens. If you are working on developing an application, it's important to use the correct status code.

4.5 What Kind of Website Is Our Landing Page?

In the case of JollyFarm's landing page, the web page is pretty simple: it only has some information about the future product and contact information. The content of the landing page won't change, regardless of who is accessing it and when. The content that exists in the server will be presented *as is*. This is what we call a static website.

A static website will return the same information regardless of who is accessing it. There's no changes to the file the server is keeping.

You can think of static websites the same way we think of basic cable television. On cable, a channel's broadcaster can't see who is watching, what they like, or anything about who's watching. The consumer, on the other hand, can't choose which programs to watch or stop a program and watch it later.

A static website can be thought of as the most simple system you can develop. A good example of a static website is a blog. A blog can list the articles available or the content of a specific article. The content will be the same no matter who or when someone is accessing it.[5] That's why a lot of blogs are made using static website technology: they are quite straightforward.

4.6 Dynamic Systems

The landing page was great to get started, but do you think something similar is what is needed for the JollyFarm's MVP? Well, let's take a look at a single requirement of the MVP: *farmers can create a new product*. A static website can't change the information, let alone handle data coming from a user. What we need instead is a <u>dynamic website</u>.

If we think of a static website as what we can see on cable television, we can think of dynamic websites as the new video streaming services. You can play the movie you like and give reviews, and at the same time the service knows who you are and can personalize recommendations for you.

The major difference between static and dynamic websites is that in the first the server has all the information that it needs to share with the client and knows absolutely nothing about who is requesting this information. Dynamic systems on the other hand are relevant when you need to interact and react to the user's input. On them, information can evolve and change over time. The vast majority of applications you find on the Internet are dynamic, and they highly rely on data.

Dynamic systems can receive and retain information from the user and return content that is personalized for them.

---

[5] In this case we are excluding comments and likes that require a more complex structure.

Servers may be good for handling HTTP requests, but they are not designed to deal with storing information as we need in a dynamic system. For this case, we need applications that are specialized in storing and retrieving data efficiently. We need databases.

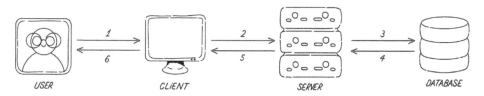

USER   CLIENT   SERVER   DATABASE

Figure 4-12. *In a dynamic website, the system heavily interacts with information provided by the user. All this information is stored in a specialized application called a database*

While the server is processing the requests and returning responses, it interacts with the database regarding data that's been available on a request. The database can store data coming from a user, while it can also quickly retrieve information the server needs to send back a response. As you can see, in dynamic systems the database becomes as important as the server.

A database is a system that is designed to store and find information.

4.7 An Introduction to Software Architecture

The type of high-level overview of a system presented in Figure 4-12 is called software architecture. The architecture of a system can change drastically depending on what is necessary for a particular system. Because of that, there is a common way of referring to parts of the system regardless of the chosen architecture. Everything that the user can see and interact with is called a <u>frontend</u>. This refers to any technology that runs on clients (desktop, mobile, tablets).

The frontend interacts heavily with what we call the <u>backend</u>. The backend is every layer that the user can't directly interact with. It contains the server that understands HTTP requests, the database infrastructure, and many more pieces that we will see later on.

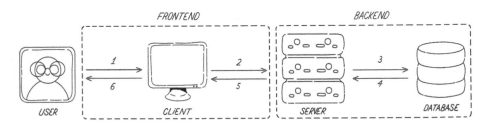

Figure 4-13. *Software architecture can change a lot depending on the requirements of a system, so it's roughly divided into a frontend (everything a user can interact with) and a backend (everything that a user can't interact directly)*

Because they solve different problems, backend and frontend technologies are quite different. They each have their own programming languages, peculiarities, and *deep* rabbit holes. That is why it's normal to find software developers that say that they are a "backend developer," rather than just a developer. However, when companies say they need a developer that understands both sides, they usually refer to this unicorn as a "full-stack developer."

For the JollyFarm ecommerce, we will need a dynamic system, because we need to handle data from both our farmers and our customers. Before we consider what options we have to build it, we should understand a bit more each part.

Figure 4-14. *We now know what needs to be done, but there's still some decisions left to be made!*

4.8 Chapter Summary

The most basic website infrastructure consists of a client (like a browser) talking to a server. Their communication must follow a protocol, which the most popular one is HTTP messages.

HTTP messages have verbs to indicate which kind of action a client wants. The most common operations—retrieve, create, update, and delete—are represented by four verbs, respectively: GET, POST, PUT, and DELETE.

In most basic systems, the server will return the information regardless of the person who is requesting the information on the client. These are called static websites. When information needs to be stored and information from the client is relevant, we need a system to store these information, called a database. Systems that require databases are called dynamic websites, as the client can change the data and the server can personalize the information depending on the client.

A high-level overview of a software system is called software architecture, and it can change quite a bit. That's why it is roughly divided into two parts:

- A **frontend** is everything that the user can interact with (such as what is shown in the browser).

- A **backend** is everything that a user can't interact with (what happens in the server).

71

4.9 Further Reading

The website *How DNS Works* explains how DNS works through some nice comic-style materials: `https://fdly.li/04-01`.

I love the explanations of technical concepts made easy by Julia Evans on her zines. If you want to learn even more about HTTP, I would recommend "HTTP: Learn your browser's language!": `https://fdly.li/04-02`.

CHAPTER 5

Frontend: The Tip of the Iceberg

A user interface is like a joke. If you have to explain it, it's not that good.

—Martin LeBlanc

The JollyFarm, as an ecommerce, will be a dynamic system. This means that it will need a frontend and a backend system. We can start by looking at what the frontend consists as you have more familiarity with it. Every website you've accessed, every mobile app you've used, and everything you interacted with while using a web application are frontends.

Frontend refers to technologies that are present on the client, which means that it is related to everything that a user directly interacts with.

Because of this intrinsic contact with users, the frontend can also be known as a presentation layer or client side.

© Leticia Portella 2023
L. Portella, *A Friendly Guide to Software Development*,
https://doi.org/10.1007/978-1-4842-8969-3_5

5.1 A Web Page Skeleton

As we've seen before, the most basic thing a server can return is pure text. But can we work using *only* text?

Let's say you have to create a sales report for one of the Jolly Co products. How does the text of such a report look like? It will have paragraphs, yes, but you also need to add a big title, small titles, bold or italic words, etc. It must have more than just words: it must have a structure that gives it meaning. Pure and simple text doesn't make information clear enough.

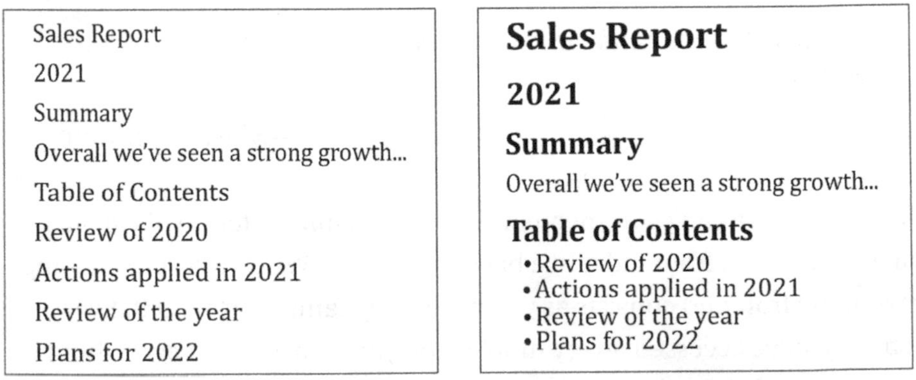

Sales Report	**Sales Report**
2021	**2021**
Summary	**Summary**
Overall we've seen a strong growth...	Overall we've seen a strong growth...
Table of Contents	**Table of Contents**
Review of 2020	• Review of 2020
Actions applied in 2021	• Actions applied in 2021
Review of the year	• Review of the year
Plans for 2022	• Plans for 2022

Figure 5-1. *Every text we produce also requires a structure so the content becomes clearer. Which of the two preceding texts is easier to read?*

In web pages, you can define a text structure using a type of language called HTML (Hypertext Markup Language).

HTML is a fairly simple language made up of elements, which can be applied to pieces of text to give them different meaning in a document (Is it a paragraph? A bullet list? Part of a table?) and structure a document into logical sections (like different title sizes).

When we said in Chapter 3 that a browser *renders* a web page, what that means is that the browser will get an HTML file and interpret the instructions and show it accordingly.

Let's see an example. In Figure 5-2, you can see that the left panel has an HTML file. This is what the browser actually gets when requesting a web page. On the right side, you can see what the browser displays. Amazing, right?

In HTML files, we encapsulate text between tags. Tags are defined by the symbols < and >. For instance, the tag <h1> opens a title of level 1, which is the biggest title we can have. Everything between the opening tag (<h1>) and closing tag (</h1>) shall be presented as a big title.

You can also see that we have a couple of other tags in the figure such as <p> for a paragraph and <ul> for starting a list and <li> for displaying a list bullet point.

You might be wondering where does this all fit on HTTP messages we've seen in Chapter 4. The same way user information travel through the request body, the HTML information travels back on the response body. Now you know the whole cycle between the request and the response!

```
1   <html>
2     <h1>Welcome!</h1>
3
4     <p>This is my first webpage.</p>
5
6     <p>I <strong>love</strong> HTML!</p>
7
8     <ul>
9         <li>These are</li>
10        <li>bullet points.</li>
11    </ul>
12  </html>
```

Welcome!

This is my first webpage.

I **love** HTML!

- These are
- bullet points.

Figure 5-2. *Example of an HTML that is sent by a server (left) and how a client presents the content (right). To be formatted, the text should be between HTML tags (defined by the characters < and >)*

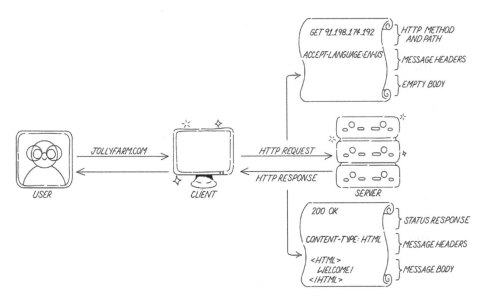

Figure 5-3. *An HTML file can be inserted on the body part of an HTTP message. The HTML file will be rendered by the browser and the cycle is complete!*

5.1.1 HTML Is a Tree!

One important aspect of the HTML structure is the relationship between tags. Consider the code you saw in Figure 5-2; you can see that the tag `<html>` contains all other tags within it and that the `<ul>` contains every single `<li>` tag.

You can think that an HTML file is a tree of tags that are related to each other. They have only one direct relationship upward (parent) and multiple relationships downward (children). In the example, the `<ul>` tag is a child of HTML, but a parent to all the `<li>`.

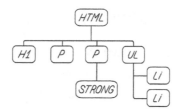

Figure 5-4. *An HTML structure is like a family tree with each tag being contained inside another and relationships being upward (parents) or downward (children)*

5.1.2 The Importance of HTML in Accessibility

One of the main concepts anyone building products must understand is: you are not your users. According to the World Health Organization,[1] 15% of the world's population have some sort of disability. While building a website using HTML, it's important to remember that you must consider the accessibility of the page for people with disabilities.

One example is people that use screen readers to read a website due to some sort of visual impairment. When an HTML page is badly written or structured, it's impossible for them to use a website. HTML tags also have additional attributes to add better description of what that tag contains. For instance, the <img> tag for displaying an image has an attribute *alt* where you can add a description of the image being displayed:

```
1    <img src="bananas.png"
2         alt="A banana bunch over a table with a green towel.">
```

Using proper HTML tags and attributes and thinking about accessibility is something that should be included from day one. It's infinitely harder to go to an older project, so we might as well start early! It's a human right to allow everyone to experience this world of software.

---

[1]https://fdly.li/05-01

5.1.3 HTML Is the Base of It All!

At this point, you can see how HTML is an interesting tool to display information. However, it's much more powerful than that! It can also receive data from a user. There are tags that are specific for handling insertion of user data. It has a lot of flexibility that allows you to say if the input should be a text, a number, a multiple choice option, and much more. Everything is defined by different tags and some definitions.

I've said before that the most basic thing a server can return is a text. That's true, but in reality, HTML is the most basic thing a server will return because it is almost impossible to show something without a minimum structure, as we've seen in the beginning of this section. And that's why HTML is the backbone of the frontend. Now that you know how the structure works, how about we add some color?

5.2 Let's Add Color!

Take a moment to go back to Figure 5-2. It's kind of boring with pure black and white, right? That's because we are using HTML and nothing more. That's why you can't really talk about HTML and frontend without talking about Cascading Style Sheets (CSS). While HTML gives the *structure* of websites, CSS helps improve its *appearance*.

The simplest way of adding CSS into a website is using a tag attribute called *style*. We could make the second paragraph of our HTML to have the color red, for instance:

```
1    <p style="color: red">This is my first webpage</p>
```

This additional configuration will now be rendered following the structure we have defined, and the text will be displayed as red, while everything else will be kept as it was before.

The preceding example is just a tiny part of the powers of CSS! Colors, font styles, divisions, columns, sizes, positions... it can do so much! It's simply amazing what you can do using CSS; the possibilities are endless.

Cascading Style Sheets (CSS) is a language that is used to change the presentation of an HTML file. It allows to change the color of text, background, size, and position of HTML tags, and it's an extremely powerful tool.

To show you how powerful it can be, look at Figure 5-5 where you can see an image that is purely done using HTML and CSS (and only that!). There are no images being used here. How impressive is this?

Figure 5-5. *An amazing drawing using only HTML and CSS made by Ben Evans. Source:* `https://fdly.li/05-02`

We've discussed the importance of CSS for giving the website its appearance, but there is a bit more to it. Think briefly how many ways you can access a website: a desktop computer, a laptop, a tablet, a phone, you can even access it by your smart TV. Now think of how many sizes of a screen these devices have: small and big phones and all the monitor sizes you can possibly think of. Websites should be able to be presented in all of those screens in a way that allows the user to enjoy it, no matter where they are accessing from.

If you ever tried to open a website in your phone and it didn't work properly, we say that it isn't a <u>responsive website</u>. CSS plays the major role in making websites responsive. Responsiveness is what allows users to have a good experience in any device they choose to use. When a developer is building the frontend of a system, they should also consider this complexity of screens and devices.

5.3 Let's Add Movement!

If HTML is a skeleton and CSS gives it skin tone, eye color, and much more, we are still missing movement! In today's websites, we don't only have web pages that display things. The third main component of frontend technologies is the programming language <u>JavaScript</u>, responsible for creating dynamic websites.

JavaScript is a programming language that allows you to implement complex features on web pages. Every time a web page does more than just sit there and display static information for you to look at— displaying timely content updates, interactive maps, animated 2D/3D graphics, scrolling video jukeboxes, etc.—you can bet that JavaScript is involved.

HTML   CSS   JAVASCRIPT

Figure 5-6. *You can think that HTML gives a web page its structure, like a skeleton. CSS gives the appearance, like colors and shapes, while JavaScript can give it dynamism!*

JavaScript, commonly referred to as JS, is the dominant programming language in the frontend. It was created for the first ever popular browser to give some dynamism to the already popular combo of HTML and CSS and is still in 2022 the most used language by professional software developers. That's why it's impossible to talk about the frontend without discussing JavaScript.

An important thing to say is that some people confuse JavaScript with Java. A popular saying is that JavaScript is to Java what ham is to hamster. Java is another—completely distinct—programming language which is very popular on the backend, while JavaScript dominates the frontend.

JavaScript is to Java what bee is to beer.

JavaScript is an interesting programming language because it's very easy to start: since it runs in a browser (and all browsers support it), basically anyone has all they need to start coding in it. Take a look at Figure 5-7. You can see the console of a Mozilla Firefox browser in the bottom, where you can run JavaScript commands. In this case, the command we typed was `alert("Hello, World!")`. Once we typed this command and pressed enter, immediately a pop-up appears where the browser is rendering a web page.

81

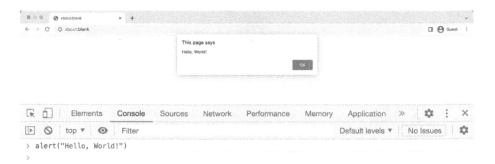

Figure 5-7. *In most browsers, if you right-click anywhere in a page and go to Inspect (Chrome) or Inspect Elements (Mozilla Firefox), you will find an area for development. You will see in one of the tabs the Console tab where you can type JavaScript commands*

Beyond being able to create a pop-up, JavaScript allows you to do a lot of things. For instance, absolutely *anything* you do in a browser is an "event"—if you move your mouse, if you type something, if you press arrow keys, if you scroll down a screen… anything! JavaScript uses these events to change the behavior of the website depending on each event.

What if we are more efficient?

Consider when you open a form and there is a field for you to add an email or add a date. It's pretty annoying when you fill a whole form only to discover later that you made a typo on your email. Do we really need to wait for the server to come back with some errors if we can avoid these errors in the first place? JavaScript allows us to add layers of validation to avoid leaking bad data to the server. This way, we avoid a pointless request to the server as well as saving the user the time and frustration of filling a whole form to only later discover a problem.

A great example of this type of validations is when you have to create a new password. Before you ever send this password, you can see a message saying that this password is not following all the criteria for a safe password. JavaScript is adding a validation to avoid creating requests to the server that it knows will fail. This can make everything more efficient!

Figure 5-8. *JavaScript allows verifications to happen on the browser, with no need of them going all the way to the server and back. Along with that, it allows HTML and CSS to be changed dynamically*

These are only a few examples of a thousand of things JavaScript can do with your website to make it dynamic. It can get much, much more powerful.

JavaScript can listen to events that happen in the browser and either add or change HTML and CSS to respond to them.

5.4 Don't Need to Reinvent the Wheel: Use Frameworks

Imagine now that you developed the complex frontend of JollyFarm using JavaScript. You run your code in production, and sooner or later someone starts complaining that something doesn't work in their browser. Another user uses a browser from the Stone Age (and they can't update for several reasons), and it doesn't support your website... you get the picture.

There are many, many things that one has to think about when developing a website. You know that each business has its own requirements, but most applications share some things, and developers don't want to reinvent the wheel every time they start a new project. For instance, when developing your frontend, you might not want to remember every single browser and version, both desktop and mobile.

To avoid reinventing the wheel all the time, a developer will typically use a <u>framework</u>. Frameworks are language-specific tools that come with tons of things prebuilt and ready for a developer to build on top of while guaranteeing some features that are needed regardless of the <u>business logic</u>.

You can think of programming languages as that big warehouse where you can find anything you need to build a house (paint, nails, tools, etc.), while frameworks are like precast building. In precast building, you can more or less adapt it to what you need in a building, and you'll still need things from the warehouse, but it makes your life easier and development quicker.

A framework is a tool that allows developers to build applications quicker, as they can mainly worry about the business logic instead of some of the implementation details.

Because of all this, frameworks are a big part of software development, and this is especially true in the frontend. It's normal for developers to talk only about a JavaScript framework rather than "JavaScript" when talking about the frontend. There are four main popular frameworks today:

- **jQuery** is one of the oldest JavaScript frameworks. Created in 2006, it is still extremely popular today, being the third most used framework in 2022.[2]

- **Angular** is also an open source framework driven by Google. It is actually a major rewrite of a previous framework, now known as AngularJS, that was launched in 2014.

---

[2] https://fdly.li/05-06

- **React** is another popular JavaScript framework that is also open source but was mainly driven by Facebook. Its initial release was made in 2013.

- **Vue.js** is a framework created by a developer that worked at Angular and decided to make a more lightweight version of that project. It was initially launched in 2013.

All JavaScript frameworks are free to use and open to contributions. If something is wrong, you can go into the code and fix it yourself. One question that might pop up is: Do we need to use them?

> *Technically, you don't need a framework. [...] You can instead choose to write all of the logic you need yourself, every time. [...] Then again, if you do use a framework, you'll be able to benefit from the good and very well tested work of dozens of other developers, who may well be better than you. You'll get to build what you want rapidly, without having to spend time building or worrying too much [...]*
>
> *You can get more done in less time, and know that the framework code you're using or extending is very likely to be done better than you doing it all yourself.*
>
> —Steve Jalim (`https://fdly.li/05-03`)

All of this makes it less common to find systems that are developed using only JavaScript and not a framework. When people want to refer to something done in pure JavaScript, that is, without a framework, they usually call it <u>Vanilla JS</u>.[3]

---

[3] In fact, there is an ironic website that describes Vanilla JS as a framework, but when you download it is just some empty files: `https://fdly.li/05-04`

If you are now wondering how to choose a framework, good! This means you are starting to understand the complexity. We will discuss more about how to choose the best tool for your project in Chapter 7.

5.5 Intelligent Clients

So far, you have learned that every time we want something different in the client (like a new web page), you need to ask for it to the server, and the server needs to send all the files every time. We can call this type of systems Multipage Applications, where every web page is a different HTML page with its CSS and JavaScript files. One thing to know about Multipage Applications is that sending all these files takes *time*!

Although we think of it in terms of being instantaneous, there is a period of time that it takes for a request to go all the way to the server and back. And with complex frontends, we aren't only sending HTML anymore, but at least one HTML file, one CSS file, and one JS file. For every request, you have at least three files traveling back from the server. Every single click, more and more files.

If your system is rather big or complex and the user has an old computer or a slow Internet, the system will make them wait for every single request. If we are talking about a website that depends on the user buying something, chances are that they will leave it before you have time to present them something interesting. In the meantime, the client is just rendering something that is being sent by the server. Could it be doing something more?

A client that just displays information is called a *dumb client*. However, as we've seen before, browsers being powered up by some JS can do much more than just displaying things. So instead of just rendering things, we can start giving more and more responsibility to clients, making them more complex and smart! That's what Single-Page Application websites do.

In SPA websites, the first time you open a website you download not only the main web page but also all the tools required to build new parts of the website. This can make the first request slower (because it's loading more information),[4] but anything after it is pretty fast! The client can request pure *data* from the server—instead of all the files—and use the tools in the client to create new parts of the website.

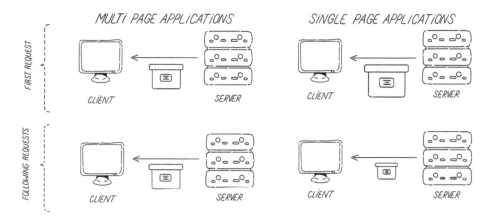

Figure 5-9. *In Single-Page Applications, the first request is slower because the server sends the HTML and the tools to build the rest of the website. However, the following requests are faster because the server can only send data, and the SPA will know how to build the information using it*

As you can see, the client is not dumb anymore. The server will continue to return data, but it will return *only* data and not whole files. Returning pure data is much faster than returning files, so the performance gain is enormous!

A way to see an SPA is when you open a website and most of its content appears on the screen, but a small part is still loading. This is a Single-Page Application that rendered the parts of the website it already

---

[4] New versions of SPAs are distributing the load across multiple requests and making even the first request fast.

has information to build, but the parts that require more wait time can be rendered at their own time. With this, the user can start interacting with the website even before everything is loaded.

You might be tempted to think that intelligent clients are the future, and thus you should use them everywhere you can. This can be true in some contexts but not always. All these concepts that were briefly explained here are extremely complex. Every time you decide to use an SPA, you are adding a lot of complexity and may decrease the speed of the project.

In software development, there is never a "silver bullet" that will work for everything and solve all your problems. SPAs are amazing if you have a lot of interactions with users and a lot of data that will take time until it loads completely. However, there are *many* other scenarios where a simple and pure combination of HTML, CSS, and JavaScript will do the trick, be fast and not as complicated.

5.6 Mobile Technologies

While JavaScript is the dominant browser language, mobile apps are a world of their own. Smartphones are divided by their operating system, and there are three main types:

- **Android**: An operating system that is mainly sponsored by Google and run on the vast majority of devices

- **iOS**: A proprietary operating system developed by Apple that can only run on Apple hardware

- **Windows Phone**: An operating system developed by Microsoft and has the smallest market share

Each one of the preceding operating systems can run applications, but they come with what's called a native programming language, that is, a programming language that can be used to develop mobile applications that the operating system will run. What happens is that the operating system is prepared to receive apps built in such languages, so they can run smoothly. These apps built in the preferred operating system programming language are called <u>native applications</u>.

Figure 5-10. *Native applications are run and distributed in the preferred programming language of the mobile operating system*

This is all straightforward, but it comes with a big problem. When you want to build an app that works in both systems, you have to build not one app, but two (or three): one for each operating system. Because of that, the apps might never be totally in sync. This can be extremely frustrating and hard to explain to a user when a specific feature works on their friend's phone but not on theirs.

As the technology evolved, alternatives started to appear where you could write the app in one programming language but still distribute it in multiple platforms, called <u>non-native applications</u>. One example of strategy is called a hybrid application, where you write the application in one programming language, like JavaScript, and then encapsulate it on the preferred programming language of the application. This way, you can write and distribute the same application at the same time regardless of the programming language of the application.

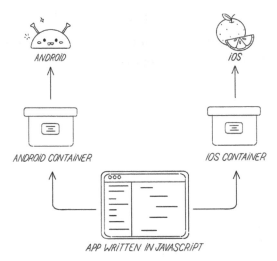

Figure 5-11. *Hybrid applications can be encapsulated into platform-specific containers and distributed in multiple platforms. This is one type of strategy for building non-native mobile applications*

You can imagine that each has its own peculiarities and trade-offs. You have to consider, for instance, that each operating system has its own designs, and users can feel the difference between the rest of their operating system and your application.

5.7 JollyFarm's Frontend

Let's refresh the requirements we have for the JollyFarm ecommerce:

- Farmers can log in to the system.

- Farmers can see a list of the products they have.

- Farmers can create a new product.

- Farmers can update information from an existing product.

- Any person can see a list of products available from all farms.

From this list, we can see that there's nothing too complex on these requirements (as MVPs should be!). Because we are talking about an MVP and there is a need to move fast, we can use a simple combination of HTML, CSS, and pure JavaScript to start. When our MVP proves to be successful and we have more funding and developers, we can iterate over it.

5.8 Chapter Summary

The frontend is the layer of software where a user can interact with. It's made of mainly three layers working together:

- **HTML** is the backbone of a website, being responsible for its structure.

- **CSS** improves the layout, adding colors, size, and life to the static and pale HTML structure.

- **JavaScript** gives power and dynamism to the website, allowing the client to have much more intelligence than it would have with only HTML and CSS—not to be confused with Java, which is a backend language.

JavaScript is a very powerful language, but it has several frameworks that allow developers to move faster and mainly worry with business logic. When JavaScript is used without any frameworks, it is called "Vanilla JS."

Mobile technologies are a world of their own, with completely different technologies from the HTML+CSS+JS combo. Typically, every operating system has its own programming language, and apps created on those languages are called *native apps*. Some technologies allow to share a single app in all operating systems, and those are called *hybrid apps*.

5.9 Further Reading

There is an infinity of topics related to frontend technologies. An open source project is mapping several technologies related to the frontend: https://fdly.li/05-05.

Stack Overflow is the main forum where developers can find answers to questions, and every year they make a massive survey about the most used technologies and frameworks: https://fdly.li/05-06.

The "Web technology for developers" written by Mozilla was a major source of explanation of some of the basic content about web development. It is highly technical and focused on learning how to code: https://fdly.li/05-07.

I would highly recommend the article "What is accessibility" (https://fdly.li/05-08) and *the guide on accessibility for HTML* (https://fdly.li/05-09) both from MDN Web Docs as starter points on accessibility.

CHAPTER 6

Backend: What's Underwater

Beautiful is better than ugly. Explicit is better than implicit. Simple is better than complex. Complex is better than complicated.

—The Zen of Python

We defined how our frontend should look like, now it's time to think about the other side! While the frontend is responsible for interacting with users and making sure they have an amazing experience with the website, the backend is responsible for implementing the business logic as well as making sure that the information is quickly accessible and securely stored.

Backend refers to technologies that are present on the server, which means that the user doesn't directly interact with it. It is also known as server-side or data layer, due to its intense relationship with data.

While on the frontend we have an infinity of JavaScript frameworks but JavaScript is the main language, it's impossible to say the same about the backend. There is an abundance of programming languages, and each

© Leticia Portella 2023
L. Portella, *A Friendly Guide to Software Development*,
https://doi.org/10.1007/978-1-4842-8969-3_6

language has multiple frameworks. Some of the programming languages for the server side are Java, Python, PHP, Ruby, Go, Kotlin, C++, etc. Even JavaScript can be used in this side!

Let's dive a bit deeper on what it means to have a server working in the backend.

6.1 A Closer Look on Servers

So far, we talked about how servers are *computers* that can return data. If we take a closer look, there's a software application running in that computer, and that application is the one listening to requests and returning responses. Because you can't have one without the other, both the computer and the software application can be called a *server* depending on the context.

You can think of a server as being a doorman. The doorman can only accept people into the building if they are listening to the doorbell. If the doorman isn't there (the equivalent of the application isn't running or the computer crashed), no one can access the building. That's why when a server is available, we say it's *listening* for new requests.

Once a request reaches the server, it checks where the request is redirected to a part of the system that can handle this request, called the endpoint. Like in the example with the doorman, when you enter to a huge business building you go to the doorman and ask which floor is the office you want to go. Each office in the building has a different purpose, but only one of them is the one you really want.

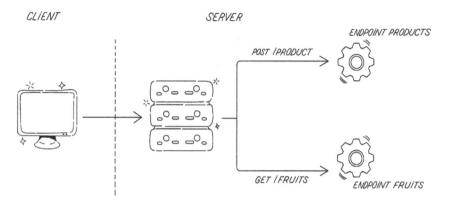

Figure 6-1. *The server will redirect the request to parts of the system that can handle this request, called endpoints*

Let's go through a single flow of creating a product and see how this request is treated in the server.

6.2 What Happens When We Create a New Product?

When a server receives a request, the first thing it needs to do is check if the request is coming from a client that can perform this request, as we've seen in Section 4.2.3.

Then the server checks if the user making the request—the farmer, in this case—is *authenticated.* If a user is authenticated, the server can continue processing the request. If they aren't, the server can redirect the user to the login page, where they can type their username and password to be allowed access to the system.

Authentication is the process to verify if a person is who they say they are.

Once those initial steps are done, the server identifies that this request is aiming to create a new product, like in Figure 6-2.

Figure 6-2. *Example of the request reaching the server*

The server now will start with the business logic such as: Does the farmer already have a product named "egg"? What if the request said that they would sell eggs per kg instead of units? Will we accept that? What if the product is being sold by units but there is no specification of how many eggs are in one unit? Should we default to one or fail the request?

After it's certain that the data coming through the request is valid, it will be packed to be sent and stored in the database (Figure 6-3). At this moment, it's usual for the system to also save information about the request being made, like the date and the user making the request.

Saving in the database is a very critical part of the process. The database, as we will see later on in this chapter, is another software system, and the server needs to communicate with it. If something goes wrong with the validation or if there is a problem on this communication, the server needs to be able to handle it, either by retrying or by letting the user know something went wrong.

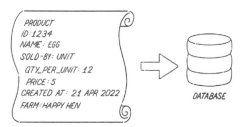

Figure 6-3. *The data from the request will be packed along with additional information and then saved to the database*

Only after all this goes well, the server can actually return with the response saying that the product was successfully created.

You can notice that for this simple request of creating a product, we have several scenarios where the response is not the creation of the product but rather something different. The default path, where everything goes right and the final result is successful, is usually called *the happy path*, but as you can see, a lot of the backend work is to deal with everything that can happen when the user doesn't go through the happy path.

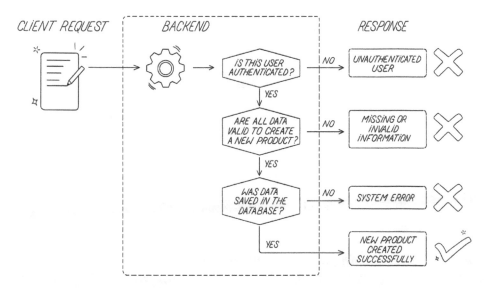

Figure 6-4. *Even a simple flow like creating a product can create multiple scenarios that must be verified!*

Although we can avoid many mistakes by adding some validation in clients, the backend must always double-check the data. We can't blindly trust any client, as things can slip by and malicious people can use this to their advantage. Someone can bypass the validation that the client imposes and send bad requests. No matter how smart your client is, the server should always make sure the request is secure and valid to proceed its tasks.

6.3 The Concept of APIs

So far, we spent most of our time discussing how a server can return an HTML page that will be rendered by the browser. The HTML page, and all the other files associated with it, has the goal of presenting information to the user, that is, a user interface.

However, in the last chapter, we've seen that with SPAs the frontend has the tools to build parts of the website in the browser. This means that the server is no longer sending the page ready to be rendered to the user. Instead, the server will send data that will then be used by the frontend. It's the frontend's responsibility to worry on how to present the data properly.

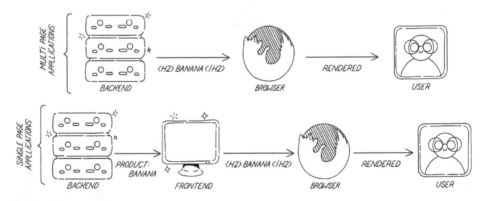

Figure 6-5. *With Single-Page Applications, the backend can send only data to the frontend, allowing the communication to be faster, as less information has to be shared between them. The frontend will use this data to create the page that will be rendered to the user*

This change from sending *user interfaces* (HTML) to sending *data* might sound simple, but it has a lot of impact. The user won't interact directly with what the server returns. Their actions like clicking a button or changing a page will be interpreted by the frontend, and when needed, the frontend will request additional data from the server.

This opens a lot of opportunities as *any* software can interact with the server. This is what we call a API.[1]

An API is a way of communicating where a server allows other software to interact with it. The responsibility of a user interface is left to other software (frontend).

APIs are the foundation of today's Internet precisely because they unlock a lot of power to web applications. We can use APIs to connect our JollyFarm system to other services so we don't have to build parts of the system we need.

We will need eventually to add payments on the JollyFarm. Payments are a very sensitive area to work with, as we need to make sure the data is securely stored, that you have a connection with a bank, that you follow all the regulations, and so on. You have to worry about so many things that it can be quite unsettling and time-consuming. Instead of doing all that, we can use a third party that will solve all these problems for us. Instead of building all the infrastructure required for receiving payments, the frontend will call your server API to send customer data. The server can call a third-party company API with the data for getting the payment. This way, you can still receive payments, but all these complexities will be handled by a third party.

---

[1] APIs can be a quite abstract concept with lots of different meanings depending on the context. I am talking specifically of Web APIs.

The beautiful part is that APIs can be used for so many things. When you log in to a service using your favorite social network, you are using an API. When you see an automated bot, that's using an API. Anytime someone wants to automatize downloading data from a website, they will likely use an API. So many more examples! An API is the basic way programs communicate data over the Internet.[2]

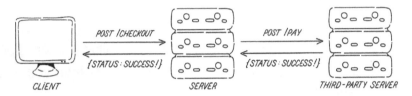

Figure 6-6. *APIs are the way a complex frontend talks to the backend, but also how the backend utilizes third-party services for doing things you don't want to build yourself. In this case, the server is calling a third-party API for the payment*

There are two main formats of structured text that can be used to share the data over the APIs: XML and JSON.

XML is similar to HTML, with each information inside tags, and the tags are defined as they need to be, to explain the information that is contained in the file, such as this:

```
1    <note>
2        <to>Amanda</to>
3        <from>Suzanne</from>
4        <heading>Card</heading>
5        <body>Thank you for dinner!</body>
6    </note>
```

---

[2] If you want to play around a fun API, check out the API built for returning information about *A Song of Ice and Fire* book series: https://fdly.li/06-01

JSON, on the other hand, is defined with a key-value structure (similar to what you've seen before in Section 4.2.3) where the key represents *what* is the data, and the value represents the data itself. You can see the same information being represented as a JSON file:

```
1   {
2       "type": "note",
3       "to": "Amanda",
4       "from": "Suzanne",
5       "heading":  "Card",
6       "body": "Thank you for dinner!"
7   }
```

You can see that both files contain the same data, but each tag on an XML file is a separate key on JSON. XML files tend to be bigger than JSON because every tag is repeated twice, but some people argue that JSON can be pretty annoying to work with. Regardless of the preference, they are both useful for building APIs.

Considering our decision regarding JollyFarm's frontend, we don't need to worry about building APIs in our backend for the MVP. As the backend will need to return the HTML files, we can start building APIs once we evolve our system. Let's assume for a moment that the JollyFarm is a success; we can then provide APIs so your customers build their own solutions on top of what we offer as a company. APIs are a fundamental part of software development, and they open a ton of opportunities that simply can't be done otherwise.

6.4 Databases

If we go back to our MVP requirements (Section 2.11), we can see that one of them is

---

Farmers can create a new product.

As we learned in Section 4.7, servers are great for dealing with requests, but they can't handle saving data. In order to allow farmers to create new products, we need a database.

A database needs to do two things: when you give it some data, it should store it, and when you ask it again later, it should give it back to you.

You can think of databases as a drawer of documents: you want it to store a document, but at the same time, it should be easy to retrieve it when you need it later on.

If you ever had a document drawer, you know that if you only throw a document in the drawer, it will be much difficult to retrieve it later, because you probably need to check a lot of documents (if not all) before getting the one you want. However, if you spend some time organizing them in smaller folders, you will spend a longer time to add a new document, but you will find it much faster the next time you need it. The same thing happens on databases. When defining the type of database that should be used, one must think if the data is going to be mainly created, mainly retrieved, or both in similar proportion. A website like Wikipedia will have many more people reading the articles than people writing them.

6.4.1 Relational Databases

A very well-known way of representing information is through a spreadsheet, dividing data into columns and rows and making sure they are consistent. In the case of the JollyFarm, we can store it like in Figure 6-7.

ID	NAME	SOLD-BY	PRICE	FARM NAME
0	BANANA	KG	5	GOLDEN SUNSET
1	EGGS	UNITS	3	HAPPY HEN
2	CHEESE	KG	6.8	COW KING
3	MILK	LITRE	1.5	COW KING
4	APPLE	UNITS	2	GOLDEN SUNSET

Figure 6-7. *A relational database allows you to easily create tables in a similar way you can do it on a spreadsheet*

Relational databases work the same way as spreadsheets, with data being distributed along rows and columns. In the preceding example, the columns are the *attributes* of a product, and every row represents one product that was stored. You can see that the farm Happy Hen sells Banana by Kg and it costs $5.

In the preceding example, how can we get information from the Happy Hen Farm? Which phone number can we use to contact them?

Our first intuition could be to just add a column called *phone* and add that information there. The problem with this is that the same information is repeated in *every* product. If the farm updates their number, we need to go over *every* product and update that information. Not very efficient. What we can do is create another table with information from the farm. Then if any information is changed, we only need to update a single place.

But then we have a problem: How to connect product and farm information? That's the beauty of *relational* databases! We can create a relationship between the two tables. We can use the ID of the farm in the "farm table" and store this ID in the products that are sold by that farm (Figure 6-8).

ID	NAME	SOLD-BY	PRICE	FARMID
0	BANANA	KG	5	0
1	EGGS	UNITS	3	0
2	CHEESE	KG	6.8	1
3	MILK	LITRE	1.5	1
4	APPLE	UNITS	2	3

ID	FARM NAME	EMAIL	ADDRESS
0	HAPPY HEN	HAPPYHEN@AMAIL.COM	1ST STREET 122
1	COW KING	CONTACT@COWKING.COM	GEORGE'S STREET 90
3	GOLDEN SUNSET	GOLDEN@ANOTHERMAIL.COM	2ND STREET 7

Figure 6-8. *A relational database allows you to easily create a relationship between tables. In one table, you can store the ID for the record on a second table*

This concept of having only one place to save information also saves space because the information doesn't need to be repeated in the table. If you update an information of a farm, you just need to change it in one place. At the same time, we can also have a better organization since product data is stored in the product's table and farm data in the farm's table.

The definition of *what* information goes in which tables is a very important thing to worry about, and it's called a database schema. Whenever you are working with relational databases, one of the first steps is to define how the data will be organized.

6.4.2 Retrieving Information on Relational Databases

Since the data is now distributed into one or more tables, we need a way to quickly access it when we need it. We also need to be able to get data from two tables that have a relationship between them. There is a special programming language that handles all the ways we want to analyze data in relational databases: SQL (Structured Query Language).

SQL is a language where you can retrieve information from one or several tables, join them all, and manipulate the data. These actions that SQL allows us to do are called <u>queries</u>.

SQL is the language that allows us to analyze data stored in relational databases.

SQL has a lot of tools and it's extremely powerful. Even if you are not a developer, you can take advantage of learning SQL in order to create data analysis for you and your business. There are other programming languages for some more high-level analysis, but because SQL is the language that allows you to go directly into the database to crunch the data, it's one of the most useful skills one can have, even if they aren't developers.

SQL is said to be a declarative language, because the way you write is by "telling" it what you want. Let's say you want to get any two products from the *orders* table. This is how you would do in a SQL query:

```
1    SELECT name
2    FROM products
3    LIMIT 2
```

This almost seems like you are writing what you want from the database in plain English! The SELECT command is where you define which columns you want the query to return. The FROM defines the table you are making the search and LIMIT restricts the number of records that are being returned.

Let's go back to the products and farms tables we saw in Figure 6-8. To retrieve data from those tables, you don't need two queries. In this case, we will add farm information by JOINing the `farms` table with the `products` table. Now we need to specify which data is coming from which table:

```
1   SELECT
2     products.name
3     farms.farm_name
4   FROM products
5   JOIN farms ON product.farm_id = farms.id
```

Because we joined both tables but selected only the product and farm names, the result of this SQL query would be like Figure 6-9.

NAME	FARM NAME
BANANA	HAPPY HEN
EGGS	HAPPY HEN
CHEESE	COW KING
MILK	COW KING
APPLE	GOLDEN SUNSET

Figure 6-9. *SQL allows us to join multiple tables, being a powerful tool for data analyses*

Relational databases use SQL as their programming language for queries, and that's why it's normal to say that relational databases are SQL databases.

6.4.3 Nonrelational Databases

Although relational databases dominated the market since the 1980s, their characteristics didn't fit some of the problems that were arriving with the newer, more complex problems of the 21st century.

Imagine that instead of building the JollyFarm ecommerce, we were building Twitter. As most social networks, the amount of data being generated at every second is gigantic and ever growing. To do so, we need a database that allows us to quickly write and retrieve millions of texts to millions of users. Since data is arriving at all times, we want to be able to change the schema as we learn more. Relational databases were not made for this job, so something else was needed. That's when NoSQL databases were born.

The term nonrelational databases (or NoSQL databases) is actually a confusing term because it doesn't explain what NoSQL databases are, but what they aren't. There are many examples of NoSQL databases, some with completely different philosophies and technologies behind. The main thing they share in common is the fact they don't rely on tables and fixed schema and that they can't be queried with SQL.

One of the most known NoSQL databases is MongoDB, which is a database that stores data as JSON documents; that's why it's called a *document database*. The following example shows the same data we've seen in the relational database but in a document database such as MongoDB. Each *document* is represented between { }, and all documents are aggregated in a list, which is represented by [ ]. In this format, each farm has its own document, and within it there is an attribute specifically for products.

```
1    [
2      {
3        "name": "Happy Hen",
4        "products": [
5          {"name": "Banana", "price": "5", "sold-by": "Kg"},
6          {"name": "Egg", "price": "3", "sold-by": "Units"},
7        ],
8        "address": "1st Street 122"
9      },
```

```
10      {
11          "name": "Cow King",
12          "products": [
13              {"name": "Cheese", "price": "6.8", "sold-by": "Kg"},
14              {"name": "Milk", "price": "1.5", "sold-by":
                "Litre"},
15          ],
16          "address": "George's Street 45"
17      },
18      {
19          "name": "Paradise End",
20          "address": "2nd Street 90"
21      },
22      {
23          "name": "Golden Sunset",
24          "products": [
25              {"name": "Apple", "sold-by": "Units"},
26          ]
27      }
28  ]
```

In this structure, the farm Golden Sunset doesn't have the attribute *address*, while the farm Paradise End doesn't have *products*. This is the freedom of schema: every document is an individual document with its own characteristics, and you can never guarantee its structure.

Another interesting type of NoSQL databases are graph databases. Graphs are a representation of networks and relationships. Think of a social network: you have people that are closely related to each other (like relatives or partners), and the same people also have connection with schools they've attended or bands they are following.

In Figure 6-10 we have a social network. The circles (called *nodes*) are a representation of something (like school and person in this case). Each node has attributes: if a person, they can have the date of birth or favorite food. Then we can create *relationships* between nodes, and those relationships also have attributes themselves. In this case, Carla is married to Chris and is friends with Elliot, while both Chris and Elliot attended the Sacred Heart school. This kind of structure can be represented in other database structures, but graph databases allow some analysis that other databases simply can't.

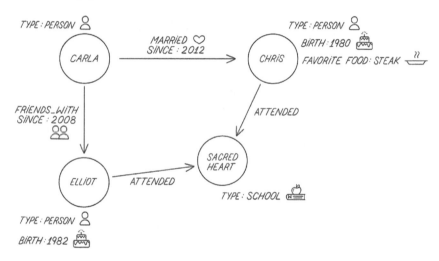

Figure 6-10. *Graph databases focus on a network. Each circle is called a node, and the arrows represent relationships, and both nodes and relationships can have attributes*

If you ever used an app to find out the best way to get from your house to a new restaurant, you have used graphs before! It's through amazing graph calculations that those apps can show you the best way of navigating through a city. In fact, all the mathematical concepts of graphs started because of a problem of how to efficiently walk a city. The graph theory was created by Leonhard Euler to solve a problem which asked if someone could visit the four areas of a city that had seven bridges without crossing a bridge twice.

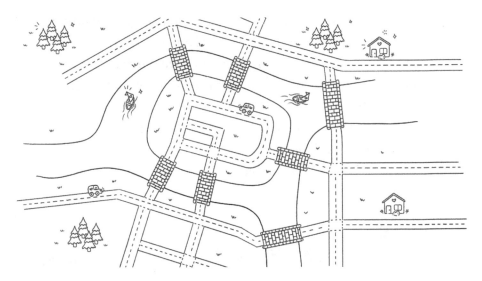

Figure 6-11. *The problem of the seven bridges gave origin to the mathematical concepts of graphs that are highly used today. If you ever used an app to find how to navigate from your house to your favorite restaurant, you have used graphs!*

Document and graph databases are just some of the types of NoSQL databases available, but there are others. It's undeniable that NoSQL databases changed the way we deal with data, and for sure many more will come as the challenges of dealing with data grow.

6.4.4 Which One to Choose?

As you now know, there are many options of databases that we can consider for the JollyFarm system, and you might be wondering which one we will use. Before we make a final decision on this, there are several other things we should consider and decisions to make. So far, we just decided the overall system of the JollyFarm system, but now it's time to make some concrete decisions. It's time for us to answer some of the big questions we will have every time we start a new project.

6.5 Chapter Summary

In this chapter, we understood the details of some of the responsibilities of the backend:

- Making sure people making requests can perform such requests (authentication)

- Validating the data being received

- Validating the data according to business logic

- Saving and retrieving data from the database

- Dealing with requests that went poorly

- Returning responses when requests were successful

As clients became more and more intelligent, servers can focus on returning only the *information* required, instead of the whole web page for display. When a server returns only information as data (instead of HTML files, for instance), they are communicating via APIs. APIs are the basis of the Internet today not only because they make requests faster, but they also allow servers to connect to other servers. This allows services to avoid building some parts and instead using third-party systems that already perform such tasks, like payments.

6.6 Further Reading

There are a couple of websites where you can see how an API behaves (with GET methods) while learning about your favorite worlds. *An API of Ice And Fire* (https://fdly.li/06-01) lets you check facts about *The Chronicles of Ice and Fire* by George R. R. Martin, while *SWAPI* (https://fdly.li/06-02) does the same for the *Star Wars* world.

Similar to the frontend, there is an infinity of topics related to backend technologies. An open source project is mapping several technologies related to the backend: `https://fdly.li/06-03`.

The guide *NoSQL vs SQL Databases* written by MongoDB (a NoSQL database) has some interesting comparisons between the two types of database: `https://fdly.li/06-04`.

The chapter "Basic Database Concepts" in the book *Relational Theory for Computer Professionals* by Chris Date has a good overview and yet goes a bit more deeply than what I wrote here: `https://fdly.li/06-05`.

PART III

Working on Software Projects

CHAPTER 7

The Big Questions While Starting a Project

It is often said that a wrong decision taken at the right time is better than a right decision taken at the wrong time.

—Pearl Zhu

Whenever a new project is starting, there are *several* important decisions that might seem trivial but can highly impact the future of the project. Although someone might jump at you with an answer for them, the truth is that it's never as simple as "use this" or "use that." As with anything in software development, there are several trade-offs that need to be made and things to be considered. Whenever making a decision, you should know about the trade-offs so they don't catch you off guard in the future!

Businesses are a volatile and dynamic environment by nature, and changes are the norm, not the exception. Even though you might be tempted to think that the MVP of JollyFarm will remain as it is for the foreseeable future, the reality is quite different. Assumptions will be challenged, ideas will be turned upside down, and you might need to rethink everything a couple of months from now. Since it's impossible to

L. Portella, *A Friendly Guide to Software Development*,
https://doi.org/10.1007/978-1-4842-8969-3_7

know everything that should and could happen in a project, you need to understand which of these decisions are the most critical. You can't avoid the downsides of a decision, but at least you know about the trade-offs you made.

When talking about decisions, one interesting way of thinking is the following:

> *Some decisions are consequential and irreversible or nearly irreversible—one-way doors—and these decisions must be made methodically, carefully, slowly, with great deliberation and consultation. If you walk through and don't like what you see on the other side, you can't get back to where you were before. [...] But most decisions aren't like that—they are changeable, reversible—they're two-way doors. If you've made a sub-optimal decision, you don't have to live with the consequences for that long. You can reopen the door and go back through.*
>
> —Jeff Bezos

To better visualize the impact of a wrong one-way door decision, imagine that you built a house. The house is almost finished: foundations are done, the walls are up, and the roof is undergoing. Then you realize that you actually wanted it 1 meter to the right. Because the foundation of the project was wrong, it doesn't matter if it is 1m wrong or it's in the wrong terrain. To fix it, you will have to demolish and start over. Some systems are like a big, expensive house. Moving 10cm is as good as throwing it away and starting all over.

As with the example of the house, *every* decision can be changed later on. The problem is that some decisions will require so much money and time that they are impossible in practice. In this chapter, we will discuss which decisions you must be aware of that can influence the present and future of your project and can be very expensive to move away from.

7.1 Which Programming Language?

As we've seen in the previous chapter, we have different programming languages, and some are very specific, like SQL exists just for querying relational databases. However, this doesn't mean that it's easy to choose the ideal programming language when designing a new system. This is probably one of the first decisions you need to make when starting a new project.

Before we discuss this question, it's important to understand that each programming language has different characteristics that make them unique in their own way. There are a lot of ways we can classify programming languages formally, but in here we will see some practical aspects.

7.1.1 Why So Many Programming Languages Exist?

There are so many programming languages that one might ask: "Why so many languages exist?". The primary goal in developing a new programming language is to make programming more efficient, so each language focuses on optimizing something.

Some languages are created to adapt and solve most kinds of problems. Python, for instance, was created to be a language that could be generally used. Other languages are created with a specific problem in mind. We've seen that JavaScript was created specifically for helping web pages be more dynamic, while Rust focuses on safety and performance, making it good for very demanding systems, such as the telecommunication industry and automation systems known as the Internet of Things (IOT).

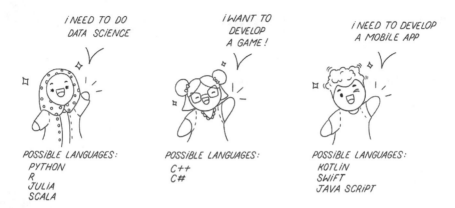

Figure 7-1. *Programming languages are created to solve a problem or optimize for something. Depending on what you need, you can narrow down the options and then choose from them*

Most programming languages are *high-level* languages. This means that the code is written in a way that is close to a human language (also known as naturals).

Take a look at the following Python code. We are telling the computer that **for** each **item** in a list ranging from **1** to **3**, the program should **print** the value in the screen. It's so close to English that reading the code is almost the same as reading this phrase.

```
1   for item in [1, 2, 3]:
2       print(item)
```

On the other side, there are programming languages that are very close to what is called the *machine language*, which is the way computers work. In these programming languages, you would have to tell the computer exactly what you need it to do, how to do it, and much, much more.

These are called *low-level* programming languages, and an example is the language Assembly.[1]

Although I just introduced this as a binary separation, programming languages can fall anywhere in the spectrum from very low level (Assembly) to less low level but still low level (Rust) to very high level (Python and JavaScript).

The more high level the language, the less worry you have with some things (that the computer requires) and the faster you can code. At the same time, because you are moving away from how the computer normally "speaks," the programming language can lose speed and other features that can be really useful in some cases. Applications that require a heavy use of the computer, such as games, normally use lower-level languages, while some websites and systems can take advantage of high-level programming languages. Nevertheless, as programming languages evolve and adapt, even this assumption becomes more and more fuzzy.

7.1.2 Programming Languages Can Be More or Less Strict

Languages also vary in terms of how they expect the code to be coded. Let's say that we need to represent the number of eggs that a customer requested. Since we can't have 2.5 eggs, we need an integer number, that is, a number without decimals. When a customer say they want 6 eggs, we will store this number in a small box, called variable, that will receive a name so we can access it later.

---

[1] I'm not even going to show some Assembly code because it really looks like a machine spat it out. If you are curious, check this website that has the same example in over 200 programming languages: `https://fdly.li/07-01`

When defining a variable to store the number of eggs, some languages require that the programmer specify that this variable is for integer numbers and integer numbers only. If we eventually change the number of eggs from an integer (6) to a decimal number like 6.25 (also known as a float number or double number) before we ever run the code, the programming language will see this change and will give a warning saying that you're doing something wrong. These are called statically typed languages.

Alternatively, some languages are completely free in what you can represent, changing the type as you like. They don't really care if you added 6 or 6.25 or even a text (called *strings*). It is your job, while writing the code, to guarantee that you won't accept 6.25 eggs or a string. These are called dynamically typed languages.

As with any other classification you can find, this is hardly binary. Some languages can be strongly types, requiring everything to have a specific type. Other languages can be more loose and let you do as you wish.

7.1.3 Programming Language Beyond the Scopes of Your Project

Another aspect of programming languages is that, by itself, the language will never contain all the tools that are required for a project. While developing a project, engineers often make use of libraries which are tools that are written in such programming language that can be plugged in to solve a problem the language doesn't.

For instance, Python doesn't have a good way to deal with matrices by default (very used in data analysis). If we want to work with this type of data, pure Python won't solve our problem. One day, an engineer wanted to do so in Python, so they created a library called NumPy (Numerical Python). You won't get NumPy by default when you install Python in your computer, but you can install this additional library and use it along with your Python code seamlessly.

The older the programming language, the higher the chances of having lots and lots of libraries for helping the development of a project in such language. This is usually the problem with new languages: you need people using the language so they can develop libraries, but you need good libraries to attract people to the language.

7.1.4 I Still Don't Know Which One to Use!

Indeed, we still haven't addressed the absolute question! Which programming language to choose is (and I guess always will be) a hard question to answer. Some studies show that if an engineer has a positive bias toward a programming language, they are more likely to use it for personal and enterprise projects.[2] Another study[3] also showed that how a language is used by other developers and companies can also impact how a developer chooses a programming language.

The problem of moving away from a language you know is similar to what happens when you learn a new natural. My native language is Portuguese, where you can ask a question by saying an affirmation and increasing the tone of the last syllable to indicate it's a question and not an affirmation. That's why you may hear many Brazilians asking "You are OK?" instead of "Are you OK?". The question will still get answers, but it's hardly as good as it could be. The same thing happens with coding. Familiarity with a programming language tends to give you *fluency* the same way that happens in naturals. The more fluent you are in a programming language, usually, the better the code.

Regardless of how a specific developer feels for a programming language, a couple of important questions to be asked before choosing a programming language for a brand-new project are as follows:

---

[2] https://fdly.li/07-02
[3] https://fdly.li/07-03

Is this programming language useful for the project you are developing?

Some programming languages have very specific purpose. It doesn't make sense to use them for another purpose where you might find a better suited language. Make sure the language can suit the problem you have at hand. Don't go hammering a nail with a screwdriver!

Does it have enough libraries for handling the problems you have?

Brand-new languages might not have a lot of libraries to help the project move faster. Without libraries, the developers will have to develop a lot of things that might be ready to use in other languages. If you don't have enough people to develop them from scratch, this is a major pain point.

Are these libraries (as well as the language) well documented?

Even if you hire the person who created the language, nobody knows everything from the heart. You need to have good documentation so it's easy to find *how* to do things and practical examples to follow. The lack of documentation can be a real problem and not an easy one to solve.

Does this language have a broad community support?

Hopefully, your project will grow and you will need to add more people to the team. Languages with broad communities can make it easier to find people to hire. You can send developers to a conference to learn how to do things better, how they can improve what you already have, and much more. Another aspect is that languages with broad communities usually get more questions and answers in development forums. Not all problems that a developer faces can be solved by documentation alone, so having questions and (*good*) answers in online forums can speed the process of fixing bugs and developing features.

Is this language close to other programming languages that the company is already using?

If your company already has a lot of experienced developers in a couple of programming languages, it makes sense—most of the time—to use similar languages. Training developers in new programming languages takes time and will not necessarily get you the best code, especially if there isn't an experienced person to help guide the beginners. Of course, if the problem is very specific and demands some specialized programming language, maybe you should consider a new language that hasn't been used before, but more often than not, using what you already have will make it easier and faster.

How hard is it for new developers to learn it?

You might have lots of senior developers on your team, but you will always need to grow some talents in house (more on this in Chapter 14). How hard is it to train new developers in this language? Will you have the senior people required to help train beginners to become fluent in this programming language? Can you afford the time it will take for them to ramp up? The project (and company) can't survive of senior developers alone!

Deciding which programming language to use is usually a one-way door decision, so making sure you understand the characteristics of the language of choice is quite essential. Just avoid choosing a trending, obscure new programming language because <big-company-name> is using it. As you now know, there is much more that should be considered.

7.2 Which Framework?

In Chapter 5, we discussed how frameworks are a huge part of frontend development. The same is also true in the backend. So the question "which framework" to use can also depend on which side you are talking about.

Of course, once you choose the programming language, you will limit your choices of framework, but this doesn't make the choice any easier! It will probably be as good of a challenge as choosing a programming language.

As we've seen before, frameworks are created with the idea of higher productivity and shorter time to market through design and code reuse, without needing to reinvent the wheel at every new project. It also helps the developer to follow a good architecture structure, helping avoid common pitfalls.

When using a framework, it can handle a lot of things that should be considered while developing a new project because the framework can handle them for you. Let's take a single example.

7.2.1 What a Framework Can Do?

Look at the following SQL code where we are **select**ing all **orders from** the **users** table but only those **where** the **username** is equal to **amanda**:

```
1    SELECT orders FROM users WHERE username = 'amanda'
```

In this case, "amanda" is a string (sequence of text) that is typed by a user. Now imagine, for instance, that instead of a user typing "amanda" or any other valid username, they type the following:[4]

Figure 7-2. *An example of a user typing SQL commands on a form in a website*

If we just take the string that the user typed and add it to the preceding SQL command, you can see that the command becomes this:

```
1    SELECT orders FROM users WHERE username = 'amanda'; DROP
TABLE users
```

This means that the original SQL command you expected to do (first one) actually became two commands, separated by a semicolon. The additional command **drop table** is the one used to delete an entire table.

---

[4] To be super accurate, the expression should end with a -- because everything after it will be ignored, like extra quotation marks.

Without much work, a malicious user deleted the whole list of users from your system! Not good. This type of attack is called SQL injection and this is a basic type of attack that should be handled. If you think this sounds too absurd to be real, in December 2021 the Internet went crazy when they discovered a similar problem with a very popular library for Java that was used for logging information.[5] Most backend frameworks will likely deal with this kind of attack, but if you decide to not use a framework, you should make sure to handle this and many other types of common problems.

While a framework will give these types of features "for free," they come with strings attached. Some frameworks are heavyweight, and they have a particular way of doing things that may or may not be aligned with the way your software will be built. They allow you to build things faster, but if you want to change their behavior, it will be trickier.

One alternative to these heavyweight frameworks is what is called *micro-frameworks*. Micro-frameworks will have a minimum structure that you can plug only the parts that you need. Need a database connection? No problem, add this package. Need a complete authorization system? Just plug it in. You can imagine it as like a plain board, where you can plug in more complicated things, but only the things you chose. This gives you more agility but also requires you to know what you need and which option is the best for you.

When deciding if you are going to use a framework or which framework to use, here are some of the questions you might want to ask:

How experienced are the people that will develop the system?

Frameworks are the result of hundreds or thousands of developers. If you have people that don't have years of experience (and sometimes even if you do), using a framework will be a good way to avoid falling into known pitfalls. The experience can also influence on how heavyweight the framework can be. Heavyweight frameworks give engineers a lot of

---

[5] https://fdly.li/07-04

tools that are already ready to go and are already optimized, while micro-frameworks might demand more knowledge of deciding the best tool for the job.

Does the framework (and programming language) have extensive support for testing?

We will talk more in Chapter 9 that testing your software is one of the most important things you should do if you want good and reliable software. Make sure that the framework provides testing tools.

How good is documentation?

Similarly with a programming language, without documentation it becomes extremely hard to use a framework, not only because it makes progress slow but also because you might not discover a lot of important features that will make your life easier. Documentation is always key when developing.

Does the framework get constant updates?

Every software has flaws. They happen. However, security flaws can be exploited by people. Using a framework that is still under active use and development will allow you to get the updates for known issues that other people have found. As with the problem on the Java library I mentioned before, if the framework is not being updated, you might need to roll up your sleeves and find and fix the vulnerability yourself!

Can you easily adapt the framework to your needs?

As we've discussed, even the most heavyweight framework may not have everything you need. The framework you choose must be adaptable and easy to create tools on top of it. This characteristic is called framework extensibility and can be quite valuable. Take, for instance, a framework that is built and designed to work well with SQL databases. Depending on how it's built, using a NoSQL database instead can be quite a challenge.

Is there a framework that most people are using? Are these companies similar to yours?

It's generally not a great idea to just copy whatever big companies are currently using just for the sake of it, but you can keep an eye on trends. Companies and developers tend to write about the tools they use, why they chose that, and what problems they face.

Also, similar to programming languages, the more people using them, the easier will be to find developers that are familiar with it, and they will more likely find more answers online. Not that this should be your only focus, but it's something that should be considered.

7.3 Which Architecture?

Another big picture decision that can be quite challenging to define is the overall system structure. You can think that, if you are building a house, deciding which tools to use (in this case, which programming language and framework) is important, but you also need the layout of what the final house should look like. The overall design of a system is called *software architecture*, precisely because it works in a similar way a physical building architecture works.

However, differently from the physical world, the architecture of a system is likely to be an evolving part rather than a static one. As new problems appear, the architecture will, most likely, need to change and adapt.

There are countless aspects of software architecture we can talk about. In fact, many things we will discuss throughout this book will be part of what consists an architecture, even if we don't talk about it as such. Let's focus, for now, on the most basic part of it: how coupled is a system.

The most straightforward way of building a system is to have all the features in a single place. In this case, every part of the system runs together, and they usually share the same database. This is what is called a monolith architecture.

Since everything runs in a single computer, it's very easy to reuse code and to create end-to-end tests, since the whole system is in one place. Also, because everything runs in a single computer, it's easy to add additional parts in production and manage it once it's live.

Now imagine that the JollyFarm was built as the monolith of Figure 7-3. Then you decide to make a major sale on Black Friday and to give massive discounts during that day. Users start to arrive and the requests start piling up. However, the delivery cost calculator uses a third-party API to estimate the costs. That API was not prepared for the load you are receiving, and the whole third-party system goes down! Our system is trying to handle this failure case, but that system doesn't come back, and this overloads the computer our system is running in. Now because of that single point of failure (delivery), we can't receive any more orders, since everything went down with it.

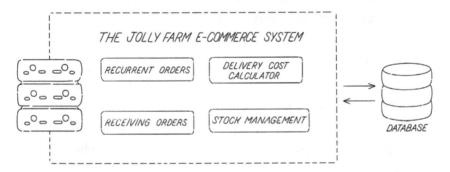

Figure 7-3. *In a monolith architecture, all parts of your software exist in a single system, and they usually share a single database*

Since everything runs in the same computer, things are connected and depend on one another, making monoliths more susceptible to a single point of failure. This means that the *whole* system should be ready for an increasing load of users (scalability), or the whole system can be down.

USING MONOLITH

1. It's easier to build, *but* multiple people might end up working in the same code.

2. Code can be easily reused, *but* if one part of the system fails, everything fails.

3. Deploys are simpler *but* the system is harder to scale.

As systems began to increase in size, one solution to avoid the drawbacks of a monolith is to break each main part of a system in a smaller service. Each system becomes responsible for a part of the product, and they are all prepared to continue working even if one of them is failing for any reason. This type of architecture is called a <u>microservices</u> architecture.

In reality, you can think that each system is a small monolith on its own. But in this case, we have many systems that talk to each other. To the external user, nothing changes between a monolith and a microservices architecture. They will still make one request to one place. Internally, however, there is a complex network of systems that call each other.

The distributed architecture allows one system to be down while other systems are still working. This is also valid for databases; since every system has its own database, a problem in one of them will only affect part of the system.

In Figure 7-4, you can see that if any of the scheduling, delivery, or inventory system is down, the order system is still up and running. The only way this architecture is completely down is if the order system is down. You can say you reduced to 25% the chance of having the system fail—only one system out of four has to crash to make the whole system crash.

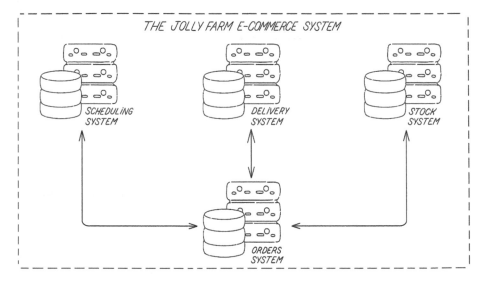

Figure 7-4. *In a microservices architecture, the whole product is divided into smaller systems that talk to each other over the Internet. This reduces the chances of the whole system going down at once*

Microservices also allow companies to have more options: each service, for instance, can be built in a programming language that works best for that problem, and each team can own their own service. With this, each team can decide when and how to deal with their service, giving them autonomy to do things as they think best. If one component becomes obsolete or can't handle the amount of users, the development team can actually develop a brand-new service and just replace it once it is ready.

Sounds nice, right? However, by adding new services, we increase the amount of work we have to do... by a lot! You will have many more services to support and manage, which requires more people and more computers.

If your software is a complex network of systems, this also has drawbacks. A great example is that it can be more difficult to find bugs. Where to search for a problem? If multiple systems keep talking to each other, how can you figure it out which system actually had a problem?

Depending on how this code was developed, it can become harder and harder to figure where something started.

Additionally, all these services have to communicate with one another. When everything is in a single system, internal communications are as simple as talking to your colleague behind you in your desk, while when we have multiple systems, it looks like communicating with colleagues that are on a different building!

You also have to understand that it can create silos of knowledge between teams. If each team has one service to take care of, they probably won't have *any* idea of how their neighbor system works. Due to the complexity of the system, it's virtually impossible for a single person to know everything. If you only have a couple of developers working on a multitude of systems, you might end up with a single person being the only responsible for a system, and that's bad. Really bad. What happens if they get sick? Or leave the company? We will talk more about these kinds of problems and decisions in Chapter 11.

USING MICROSERVICES

1. Easier to scale with the number of customers *but* increases the complexity and costs

2. Improves team autonomy *but* creates silos of knowledge (each team only knows about their piece)

3. Allows systems to continue to run even if parts of it fail *but* makes it harder to find bugs

Microservices give you a lot of possibilities and can help scale systems, but they come with consequences—complex and expensive consequences. Several benefits, several additional worries.

7.3.1 You'll Never Get a 100%

Everything in software development is a trade-off. Most of them will probably be a one-way door because changing from one solution to another is very costly—possible, but still expensive.

When deciding which architecture to consider, remember a famous phrase:

> *Premature optimization is the root of all evil.*
>
> —Donald Knuth

Don't try to replicate the structure of *<big-company-name>*. You won't have the same quantity of engineers, amount of money, or even amount of users. It's important to plan for the near future and current demands but still trying to allow room to change and evolve as the system grows.

There are strategies to start small and simple by building a monolith that will later be improved and broken into several microservices. Architecture is not a static decision, it can change and evolve over time. If your system is having scaling problems because you have too much users, you will then have the time (and money) to invest in improving the architecture. This is not necessarily true from day one.

Beyond the decision monolith vs. microservices, there are several other architectural decisions that will need to be made. More important than finding the "perfect" one, you should focus on understanding the priorities of the business, so the architecture can be designed optimizing what actually matters.

What's more important: a fast response or making sure everything is OK before responding?

Let's say two users simultaneously bought the last single avocado available in stock. If you want a fast response (to guarantee satisfaction), the system can respond to both clients that they bought the avocado, and later on you can handle the problem of where you will find one avocado for one of them. However, if you are receiving a payment, you really want to make sure the payment went through before returning any messages, even if it takes a while. Which parts of the system you expect a fast response, even if it's not a consistent one, and which parts can handle a wait time to make sure everything works?

How will your users behave typically?

If your farm is in the United States and you only sell turkey, you can expect that you will have a high demand period (Thanksgiving), while the rest of the year will be roughly a similar amount. If you sell a product that is consumed during the whole year, you can expect a steady demand all through the year. How do you imagine the users will typically behave? In the first case, the system must be ready to have a high demand in a single day, while in the second case, you can afford to have a system that doesn't handle so many requests simultaneously.

Where will your system run?

Every time we talk about *running* a program and *processing* and *analyzing* data, we are talking about money. Computers have a cost, and fast computers have higher costs. Do you want to build the infrastructure on your own? Will you use cloud computers that are guaranteed by a third-party company? Make sure you know the budget you have for this infrastructure and the restrictions you might need to impose.

Some countries have what is called a *data locality* rule. This means that the data of a customer can't leave the country, they should always transit and be stored in the country. Make sure you understand the legal requirements that your business is subject to, since some of them can affect the architecture you are considering.

How many users do you imagine the system will have in the first few months? And years?

A good exercise is trying to imagine how many users you might have in a certain period of time. If your business is too uncertain and fragile for this exercise, you shouldn't worry too much about it early on.

As we've seen before, optimizing a software before it is needed often causes more problems than brings solution. I once worked on a very field-specific software where the engineers were deeply worried about optimization and were spending a lot of time discussing how to improve their design. I arrived in the project and quickly became confused: Why were we working on this at such early stages of the project? I asked them how many users we could have in the best-case scenario, if all possible users in the country were using that service. The answer was 20,000 users. Although it seems a lot, 20,000 users are not a gigantic number for a software. For this project, there was absolutely no need to worry about it in that point of the project because even in the best-case scenario, the number of users was low. We were not building the next social network that could have potentially millions or billions of users. We were building software to—at the best-case scenario—a few thousand people.

As we talked a lot in this chapter, everything depends on your business and team structure. Every time you are faced with a decision, make sure you are doing the best for now but leaving room for growth in the future. You should try your best to make good decisions today. If demand comes later, when your software is a hit and you need to handle millions or billions of users, you will have money and engineers to figure out how to fix what is not working anymore.

7.4 Which Database?

Here is another important decision to make at the beginning of a project! Databases are also part of the architecture you need to define early on. Choosing a database that doesn't suit some of your specificity can give you a lot of headache down the line.

How is your data structured?

Depending on the type of your business, you know the typical structure and schema of the data you will have. You will probably know if they are or aren't likely to change over time. A structured data allows you to use either a SQL or a NoSQL database, but an unstructured data will be hard to deal with in a SQL database, although you can find alternatives to make it work. PostgreSQL is a famous SQL database that also allows you to store data similar to what you find in NoSQL databases. Make sure you understand how your data typically behaves and what your priorities are.

How is your data relationship?

In the farm ecommerce, orders have a strong relationship with customers and products. One user can have multiple orders, and each order can contain many products. An SQL database can handle relationships like these really well, and it will probably be the best choice in this case. If you need to store things that don't have a relationship with one another, a NoSQL might be better suited. Make sure you think about the data you want to store and how they relate to each other.

How often will you input or read data?

NoSQL was built for high amount of use. Since you don't have to organize your data into multiple tables and follow schemes and validations, the database allows you to have a faster response. This doesn't mean that all NoSQL databases are much faster than SQL databases at all times.[6] As with most things on this field, there are trade-offs to be made. If you understand what you need from your database, it can help choose one that will be best at what you need it most.

Do you have specific needs?

As we've seen in Section 6.4, some databases have specific uses, as graph databases. When considering the types of data you have, also consider the types of specific needs that you might encounter, such as

- **Spatial distribution**: Data that is tightly coupled with position in space has some peculiarities that need special types of databases and queries, such as[7] PostGIS, ArcGIS, and QGIS.

---

[6] https://fdly.li/07-05

[7] GIS means Geographic Information System, which is a system focused on spatial data.

- **Graph relationship**: When the relationship between entities start to become complex and even the relationship has attributes that should be stored, you might consider a specialized graph database, such as Neo4J and Titan.

- **Full-text search**: In some cases, you need the ability to search for keywords inside texts and allow to search for correlated words. For instance, if a user searches for "tomato," they might mean "potato." Databases that allow full-text search can do these kinds of searches by similarity.

Do you need guarantees of consistency?

Imagine that someone is paying an order: money is moving from the person account to your account. This is the kind of logic where either *all* things happen or *none* happens; otherwise, you are left with an inconsistency: money moved out but didn't arrive anywhere. This is called an atomic transaction. This is a characteristic that is only available in SQL databases, so if you need this kind of consistency, you better go with an SQL database.

How do you want to pay for it?

Databases can demand a lot of work to correctly maintain them. Not only you need to make sure they are available so they are able to store and retrieve data, but you also need to guarantee that the data is replicated somewhere else (backup) in case something goes bad. You don't want to lose all your data when you have a problem!

Contrary to (most) programming languages and frameworks, databases can be paid and be quite expensive. Some databases can be self-stored, but the companies might offer paid infrastructures ready to use. Make sure that you choose a database that is good for your business but that you can afford at the end of the day!

How is the programming language support?

You need to be able to communicate with the database you choose. Most programming languages don't come with support to database communication by default, so people develop libraries to do so. You need to check if the programming language has support for communicating with the database you chose; otherwise, it's probably not worth it to create such library.

7.5 Don't Give Answers to Questions That Weren't Made

As you can see, there are several questions one should consider while making the first decisions of a project. Defining which technology to use before understanding the problems you're trying to solve is like trying to define an answer to a question that wasn't made.

It's not unusual to see people getting "hyped" by this or that technology and deciding that their company should use it, without ever knowing if they have the need for it. At one company, a director decided they needed to change their architecture to use big data. Big data, by definition, should be used when you have so much data that you can't store or process it in a single computer. It requires an extensive infrastructure and a shift of mindset by the developers. The problem was that the data they had wasn't even close to being big enough to justify that. The developers spent tons of time just trying to reverse-engineer the small data into a big thing that could then use the complex infrastructure the director wanted. In this case, the consequence was an enormous amount of wasted time and resources. I can also say for sure that the developers were frustrated for spending so much time on something that was, in essence, useless. Maybe they could at least learn something from it, but nobody likes to work on something useless.

What can happen as well is that because they have spent so much time and money in this brand-new technology, they will try to make it worth the effort. Since it was built with no particular problem in mind, that solution will solve nothing. Then the teams will spend months or even years fighting these technologies just because nobody wants to just admit defeat and start over with the correct approach.

Although you might hear about all the shiny new features that someone is being pumped about, make sure you are asking the right questions and that they can solve a use case you have or will have shortly. It's really easy to find yourself going through a one-way door and realizing it when it's just too late.

7.6 Let's Answer Some of These Questions!

We already defined what we will use for the frontend, so time to answer some of these questions for the backend!

For the JollyFarm MVP, we will use *Python*[8] as the programming language. First of all, Python is a very mature programming language with an extensive community of developers working on it. It's a multipurpose language which means that it will have all the tools we will need for this project. Since it's been around for a while, it has extensive documentation, robust libraries, and broad community support. There's also the advantage that it is an easy language to learn and the developer (me) knows it really well!

Python offers me a couple of frameworks, but for this particular case, I will use *Django*.[9] Django is also a framework that has been around for a long time and has extensive support. It has one of the most impressive documentations of a project like this, and it has been used by some major

---

[8] https://fdly.li/python
[9] https://fdly.li/django

companies, like Instagram and *The Washington Post*. As this is a very complete framework and we have an MVP with few people working on it, it will be perfect for what we need. We will start with a monolith. Let's keep it plain and simple for now!

Finally, we will use an SQL database. Our system expects data to be very structured as products share similar attributes like name and price. Instances of data all have a strong relationship between them: farmers have multiple products, customers create orders, orders have products attached, and so on.

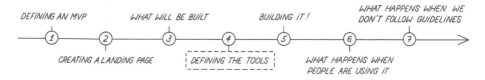

Figure 7-5. *We just defined the tools we will use throughout our project, and now we need to learn how to build it!*

7.7 Chapter Summary

When starting a new project, you need to make several decisions that will be too expensive to change in a later moment. At this point, it's important to think about the problems you're trying to solve, the expected behavior of your users, and what resources you have to work with. In software development, everything is a trade-off, and there isn't a definitive answer one can give you, so understanding exactly what you are committing to and what the possible cons of your decisions are can help you at least not be caught by surprise if you ever face them.

7.8 Further Reading

The third chapter of the book *Python Web Frameworks* by Carlos de la Guardia, called "What's the Right Framework for You?", had some interesting comments that made me think a lot.

The blog post "How to choose a framework" by Christian Varisco was also another good read: `https://fdly.li/07-06`. I also enjoyed a similar blog post focused on programming languages called "How to Choose A Programming Language for a Project" by Jun Wu: `https://fdly.li/07-07`.

A lot of the database questions were distilled from a very technical book called *Designing Data-Intensive Applications* by Martin Kleppman. This book is amazing if you want a deep-down explanation on things, so it's definitely not beginner friendly: `https://fdly.li/07-08`.

Martin Fowler defends that you should always start with a monolith architecture first and, only when you actually need, move to a microservices approach on the article called "MonolithFirst": `https://fdly.li/07-09`.

CHAPTER 8

How Do We Build Software?

Change your opinions, keep your principles; change your leaves, keep intact your roots.

—Victor Hugo

So far, we spent a long time on decisions and work that happen before a single line of code is ever written. We have the requirements for the MVP, we know the tools, now comes the fun part! It's time to start building it. To do that, we need to have developers working together toward common goals. How does this typically work?

8.1 The Old Way

Once upon a time, the development process was a straightforward process. The requirements were defined by business people, and some experienced developers (called software architects) would create the detailed definition of what needed to be done. They would create a document that would have all the answers and detailed plan on how to build this. After this document was ready, it would go to developers that were going to do the coding part. Once the code was done, they would gather all changes in one release version of the software.

© Leticia Portella 2023
L. Portella, *A Friendly Guide to Software Development*,
https://doi.org/10.1007/978-1-4842-8969-3_8

This is a linear approach to develop software known as the <u>Waterfall methodology</u>. It considers that each step depends on the things that were produced by the previous steps. This methodology relies mainly on the idea that if we find problems early in the process, they are exponentially cheaper than if we find them later in the process.

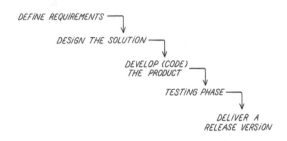

Figure 8-1. *The Waterfall methodology is a linear process where each step depends on the deliverables of the previous step*

This process—from requirements to release version—could take a long time. This is a problem: first because it's really hard to define the proper software requirements needed to solve the user's problem in its entirety months or even years before the software is available to users. Also, this process involved several people and tons of written documents. All definitions and problems should be addressed and defined before any code has been written.

This methodology faced several criticisms. It's an overweighed process, where a lot of time (20–40%) is spent just in the first two steps of defining requirements and designing the solution, while the coding itself had a limited time in between processes. Also, what would happen if something was wrong in the development phase? Where can we go back and rethink what we know!?

If you consider that software in the old days had releases that could take many years, you can imagine how hard it would be to define everything that should be worked—and how it should be worked—years in advance. Nowadays, even a couple of years can mean a huge difference, and new technologies that change the reality are adopted smaller and smaller amounts of time. TikTok, one of the newest social networks, reached over 50 million users in less than five months since its release.[1] If a single technology can change behavior and impact the world in just a matter of months, how can we create full finalized solutions years in advance?

There is also a huge criticism on this methodology because it heavily relies on the fact that a user knows what they want from the start and the requirements phase is just a matter of making these wants explicit. This isn't true in the majority of cases. What happens if the software goes to the user months (or years) after the requirements phase and they realize that this is not what they wanted? What now? A lot of time and money were spent on something that wasn't what they want. And as the methodology itself states, changes at later phases of projects are more costly than in the beginning.

8.2 There Must Be a Better Way!

While the Waterfall methodology tries to make requirements static, the reality is that

> *In building business software, requirement changes are the norm, the question is what we do about it.*
>
> —Martin Fowler

In 2001, a couple of developers, tired of the heavyweight and bureaucratic processes, decided to create the Manifesto for Agile Software Development, often called simply as the Agile Manifesto. The Agile

---

[1] https://fdly.li/08-08

Manifesto was a document that created the <u>Agile</u> philosophy, which is the basic philosophy of building software nowadays.

The idea behind the Agile movement was to change the focus from extensive documentation of requirements to delivering software to users as soon as possible and quickly iterate on it based on the feedback. Instead of fighting changes, it embraced change as the default way of the world. The manifesto is composed of four major values:

Individuals and interactions   over processes and tools

Working software   over comprehensive documentation

Customer collaboration   over contract negotiation

Responding to change   over following a plan

This movement doesn't discard the importance of documentation or making plans, but it shifts the priority on the things that matter the most. The difference is avoiding massive changes and focusing on quickly delivering small and incremental changes (known as <u>Continuous Delivery</u>). The main idea was to make the cycle between planning, development, and production as small as possible, focusing on getting feedback that the product is going in the right direction quickly. This idea became sort of a mantra of modern startups:

Fail fast, fail often

The sooner you get feedback, the sooner you can correct the plan and aim to a better direction. The overall process, however, isn't a complete blind process. Companies and teams still plan for the future, but the user gets the central stage, helping build the *right* product. The short cycles allow for companies to move fast and build the right thing, but don't lose too much time and money if they happen to fail.

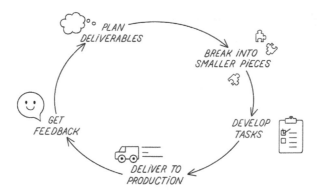

Figure 8-2. *The Agile philosophy focuses on small cycles so feedback can be obtained early and the project can quickly respond to it*

There are several different methodologies that follow the Agile philosophy but with different approaches. Regardless of the specific methodology used, it is undeniable that Agile is the industry standard today. Even in this book, you will be introduced to a series of concepts that are present as the industry standard but are, in some way, related with Agile principles. It became difficult to talk about modern software development without talking about the multitude of facets that the Agile Manifesto introduced.

Let's take a look at some of the most common Agile methodologies:

Scrum

Scrum works with small iteration, and each one is called a sprint. A sprint can vary from a single week to a whole month, with two weeks being the most common. This methodology is also heavily based on meetings, also known as ceremonies. Scrum defines four meetings:

- **Sprint planning**: This meeting happens every beginning of a sprint and aims to answer what will be done in this period of time and how it will be done.

- **Daily Scrum**: A 15-minute meeting where the development team will state what will be done in the next 24 hours.

- **Sprint review**: This meeting happens at the end of a sprint. The team evaluates what was achieved and sees what will spill over to the next sprint.

- **Sprint retrospective**: The moment where the team will evaluate what went well and what can be improved for the next sprint in terms of people and processes. It happens after the sprint review.

One of the downsides of the Scrum methodology is that there are a lot of meetings during a small period of time that some people report to be too much. A 2020 survey reported that at least 27% using a hybrid between Scrum with other methodologies or multiple methodologies at once.[2]

Extreme Programming (XP)

Similarly to Scrum, Extreme Programming works with the concept of iterations. The idea is that at the end of every iteration, there is a working and functional software. Every quarter, the team gets together to do a long-term planning and discuss internal and external problems they are facing.

The XP has its own 13 principles, lots of them focused on the team. Some are very basic such as the requirement that the whole team should sit in together in the company office, while others are very technical such as pair programming and test-driven development (which you will learn about in the next few sections and chapters).

---

[2] This survey had a large amount of Scrum master respondents (39%), a role that is specific of the Scrum methodology. This might be biasing the research toward reporting a higher use of pure Scrum (58%), so I wouldn't be surprised if the number of hybrid methodologies was higher. https://fdly.li/state-agile-2020

Kanban

Kanban, on the other hand, doesn't have clear iteration cycles. Based on a methodology for a Japanese manufacturing industry in the 1950s, it is a much lightweight tool than XP and Scrum. It gives a general idea on processes that help the team, but not exactly how to apply them day to day. It is mainly focused on helping a team improve the way they build software. There are three main ideas behind Kanban:

- **Visualize the workflow**: The work should be split into small tasks, where each one will take, ideally, less than a day to be executed. Then each task and its progress should be visible to other teammates, like post-its in a wall.

- **Limit work in progress**: There must be a limit to how many tasks may be in progress at one time. If there are more people than the limit, the team should work together, in pairs.

- **Measure the time it takes to complete a single item**: The idea is to optimize the process to make the time to complete each task to be as small and predictable as possible.

Due to its simplicity, Kanban is a commonly adopted method, but it lacks some supporting practices, and thus it's sometimes used with other methodologies forming a hybrid methodology.

8.3 Shared Strategies

Most teams I've worked with have never declared explicitly which methodology we were using. We used some mix of multiple methodologies and added or removed strategies as we needed them. The most important shared strategy between all Agile technologies is *testing*. Testing is so important that I dedicated a whole chapter to it (Chapter 10)!

8.3.1 User Stories

One concept that is shared in a lot of the Agile methodologies is the concept of user stories. We talked in Chapter 2 of user and system requirements as descriptions of features that you might want in your software. Instead of dealing with requirements as we've seen previously, a user story is written the following way:

As a *(type of user)*, I want to *(specific action I'm taking)* so that *(what I want to happen as a result)*.

We could use this structure to define a user story for the JollyFarm app:

As a *farmer*, I want to *log in* so that *I can access the system*.

Instead of focusing on what the system should do, user stories focus on what the user will see and do. It's an effective way of thinking about requirements and value from the perspective of the user.

8.3.2 Kanban Board

Regardless if the team prefers user stories or system requirements, they both need to be broken in smaller tasks, preferably tasks that can be done in a single day. Although the Kanban board is a clear trait of the Kanban methodology, it's vastly used by development teams. The idea of the Kanban board is to visualize the work being done. The team can easily see the status of each task. It also helps showcase tasks that are being blocked, so leaders can act on unblocking it as quickly as possible.

The *TODO* column presented in Figure 8-3 sometimes is called a backlog, and it contains all the tasks that we would like to do. The higher in the column, the higher is its priority. The *Doing* column is sometimes called a Work in Progress (WIP). When a task is taken by someone in the team, the card moves from the TODO column to the Doing column.

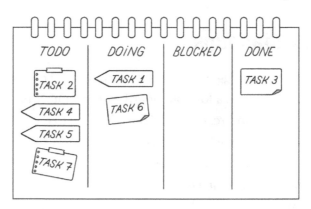

Figure 8-3. *A Kanban board is used to make it fairly visual the development of the small tasks that compose a project*

If a developer can't execute a task for any reason, they will move it to the *Blocked* column and can potentially take another task from the TODO column in the meantime. A task can be blocked because it may need more business details or is dependent on a task that is being done by another person or team, because it requires the action of another developer, etc. There are numerous reasons why a task might be blocked, but having tasks in the Blocked column is a way to get attention from the people whose job is to make sure the team doesn't get blocked.

Tasks may be added on the Backlog by a manager, by developers, or by other teams. They can be the result of a requirement being broken down in tasks, a bug that was caught, or even some feature that you might want to work on someday. As long as someone organizes the task's priorities and makes sure the team is working in the important things, the Kanban board works really well.

A team can use a wall and sticky notes to create a visible board, but some teams prefer a software version that allows them to extract metrics and reports more easily. There are a couple of software like this, and they can vary from very straightforward to highly complex, such as Trello, Monday, and Jira. GitHub and GitLab have tasks, typically called *Issues*.

8.3.3 Daily Standups

As teams get bigger and bigger, it becomes hard to keep up with what is happening. Even if you use a Kanban board, you probably need to check it multiple times a day and read every ticket to be up to date. The daily standup is a small meeting where everyone in the team shares what they did in the previous day and the plan for the day. The idea is that in a few minutes, everyone in the team gets enough information to know what is happening and what are the problems their colleagues are facing.

The event is called a standup meeting, precisely because it should be done with the team standing. If the meeting is long enough for you to feel that you need to sit down, it's wrong. The updates should be quick and concise. If anyone needs more information, they should discuss it after the meeting, so that only the people involved in the decision are there, not wasting anyone's time.

8.3.4 Pair Programming

One of the hardest problems to solve is sharing knowledge among developers. There is always a trade-off between moving fast, by giving a task to someone that already knows how to do it, or moving a bit slower but sharing context.

One might be tempted to always move fast by giving similar tasks to the same person, but the truth is that this isn't a smart move. What if that person gets sick? Goes on parental leave? Takes vacation? Decides to quit?

We need to break the knowledge silos as much as possible, so everyone has a little context on everything that is the team's responsibility, and avoid the deep terror of getting the one critical person not being available for any reason.

One way of doing this is by *pair programming*, a practice that emerged from the XP methodology. Pair programming essentially means that two developers will write code together on one machine solving a single problem.

In a pair programming, the developers take a single computer. One of them, the Driver, will take the lead and will be the one typing and making the changes; the other will be sitting next to the first one and will be the Navigator. If the Driver has more experience, they could do things while telling the Navigator what they are doing and why. If the opposite is true, the Navigator can explicitly tell the Driver what to do. This should be done during a certain amount of time (10–20 min), and then they should switch roles.

This technique is effective as long as both developers are focused. You need to have and develop good communication, be ready to receive quick feedback on your code, and be respectful to one another.

Pair programming can be used in a couple of moments:

- **Sharing knowledge**: Allowing a developer that is missing context in some part of the codebase to learn from someone that has experience in that area.

- **Learning**: When a new developer joins the team, especially if they are early in their careers, they can be paired as a way of learning the codebase and getting comfortable asking questions and working with their colleagues.

- **Work on a complex task**: Some tasks can be quite daunting. Working together will allow developers to carefully think about the strategies and possible problems.

For some people who are unfamiliar with this process, they might think that this is a waste of time, as you have two developers in a single task. There's a tweet that captures the essence of it:[3]

> A: But if all of our programmers are pairing, won't they write half as much code?

> B: No. Hopefully they'll write even less than that

> —Ben Rady

There's more to developing systems than lines of code. Lines of code are not indicative of how productive a developer or a team is. In fact, if you can solve a harder problem in less lines of code, even better! This means that we found a simpler way of solving it, and the team has less code to maintain in the future. We also have to consider that sharing knowledge between the team is invaluable and can only be beneficial.

8.3.5 Continuous Delivery

If we want software to be out in production as quick as possible, we can't really wait for massive releases to be packed together. What we need are small incremental changes that can always be—safely and reliably—deployed to production as soon as they are ready. This is the idea of Continuous Deployment.

The only way of safely and continuously adding more code to production is to create automated processes that guarantee system quality at all times, preventing bugs to go into production as best as possible.

Continuous Deployment also means that the code must be constantly added to the main codebase in small incremental changes. This is called Continuous Delivery (CD). And in order to have a good flow of code, you

---

[3] https://fdly.li/08-01

also need to automatize checks, tests, and anything we can do to make sure that all the small incremental changes are reliable and secure and will not break everything! This is the role of Continuous Integration (CI).

It's impossible to talk about Continuous Delivery without talking about Continuous Integration, and that's why we usually talk about CI/CD rather than just one or the other.

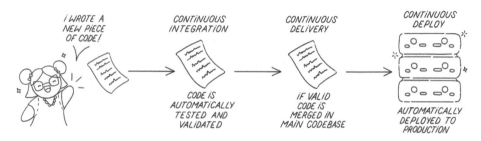

Figure 8-4. *In order to quickly iterate on customer feedback, we need incremental changes that can be constantly added to the codebase and quickly deployed to production. We can only do that with a pipeline that guarantees that we are not breaking everything all the time!*

Although not ideal, you can have Continuous Delivery without having Continuous Deployment. If someone needs to push a button to deploy, it's not Continuous Deployment. It may be *almost* as good as the automated version, but it will never be quite as if you need someone to keep an eye on things; it means you are prone to human errors.

8.4 Beyond Agile

The Agile philosophy is the most known philosophy out there, but newer ideas are surfacing as time goes by. One of the most known modern ideas on software development is the Lean Principles. These principles

153

are an adaptation of the Lean Thinking methodology used by the Toyota Production System for improving their car factories. The main idea of Lean Thinking was to eliminate waste, which was anything that doesn't create value to customers. Toyota transferred the concepts from manufacturing to product development, making sure that the product is finished as fast as possible because all the work that goes into development is not adding value:[4]

> *Every bit of code increases complexity and is a potential failure point. There is a great possibility that extra code will become obsolete before it's used; after all there wasn't any real call for it in the first place. If code is not needed now, putting it into the system is a waste.*
>
> —Mary and Tom Poppendieck

Some of the principles are very common, such as *empower the team* and *amplify learning*, while others are less intuitive like *decide as late as possible*. The idea of the latter is that if you can postpone a decision, you should do it, because over time you will have more information to reach a better outcome than what you have today.

At the end of the day, the most important thing is for teams to be able to develop the best way for them to work together. No single methodology will solve all the problems, so, ultimately, each team will be able to tell if things are working, and they should be allowed to change and adapt the methodologies to their reality.

---

[4] From *Lean Software Development: An Agile Toolkit.*

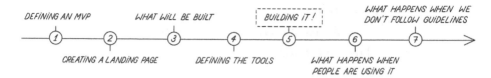

Figure 8-5. *We just learned how teams typically build software, and it's time to roll up our sleeves and understand what we should consider while building our software system*

8.5 Chapter Summary

The Agile philosophy is the standard way of building software. The main idea is to get software to customers as soon as possible, so they can give feedback and we can quickly respond to them. The shorter the cycles, the better we can avoid delivering things nobody wants. There are many methodologies that apply these ideas, but most of them share similar practices such as

- **User stories**: Defining features focusing on what the user wants to do.

- **Kanban board**: A board where teams can easily see which tasks are being worked on and which ones are blocked. They can also see the list of tasks in the order of priority they should be done.

- **Daily standups**: Quick meetings where the team shares the updates and blockers.

- **Pair programming**: When developers work together in a feature or bug so they can learn from each other.

- **Continuous Delivery**: Code is delivered in small incremental pieces that is automatically validated and deployed to production.

8.6 Further Reading

The official website of the Agile Manifesto is pretty small, so it's worth the read: `https://fdly.li/08-02`.

I really liked the book *The Nature of Software Development* by Ron Jeffries (one of the developers that signed the original manifesto). It talks about Agile principles in fun and easy way to understand: `https://fdly.li/the-nature`.

The talk "Agile is Dead" by Dave Thomas is a very blunt and interesting talk about the problems of what the industry transformed the original principles: `https://fdly.li/08-03`.

The book *Lean Software Development: An Agile Toolkit* by Mary and Tom Poppendieck is an excellent reference on the Lean Principles: `https://fdly.li/08-04`.

I liked the article "On Pair Programming" by Birgitta Böckeler and Nina Siessegger that goes into great detail on the advantages of pair programming and the different styles of pair: `https://fdly.li/08-05`.

The Phoenix Project by Gene Kim, Kevin Behr, and George Spafford is a great (and fun) read about the struggles of a manager that is pulled in to a late project where everything is on fire. The book talks about Agile and Lean Principles being applied on a "real case" dumpster-fire project: `https://fdly.li/phoenix`.

Henrik Kniberg made a video about how *Spotify Engineering Culture* works, and it shows a bit the evolution from how they started with Scrum and moved to something more loosely but still following Agile practices: `https://fdly.li/08-06`.

I also enjoyed the post "Continuous Delivery vs. Continuous Deployment: What's the Difference?" by Harness: `https://fdly.li/08-07`.

PART IV

What You Should Consider When Building Software

CHAPTER 9

Building Today Thinking of Tomorrow

The true test of good code is how easy it is to change it.

—Martin Fowler

Software is never done. There is always a new feature that was requested or a new bug that needs to be fixed. In reality, the developer will spend the vast majority of time not writing code but reading it.

As with any natural system, a software project tends to chaos unless we actively fight against this. This is because the more chaos we have, the worse it gets. That's why projects lose traction, budgets overflow, and stress piles up.

Even though we are just starting the JollyFarm system, we need to worry about how to make the code easy to work with in the future. We can't afford to only care about good code when something is already done. Thinking of the future might cost speed development today, but will guarantee a future with less worries, less pain, and more speed to add new features.

Maintainability is an abstract characteristic of software projects that states on how easily it can be changed and/or evolved with time.

© Leticia Portella 2023
L. Portella, *A Friendly Guide to Software Development*,
https://doi.org/10.1007/978-1-4842-8969-3_9

Maintainability is what makes life better: adding new features is easier, finding why a bug is happening is peaceful, and everything is much, much cheaper than otherwise (in time, stress, and money). As Micah Godbolt said,[1] "good code never happens by accident." This should be considered as critical as delivering features and making customers happy.

Although it's an extremely important concept to consider when developing a project, it's also the easiest to let go when time is short and deadlines were missed. It's the first thing that we abandon, because its effects can take time to appear. As the team try to move faster, they leave the code in bad condition, which makes it harder to add new features, which makes things slow, which doesn't give you a lot of time to improve the code... you get the idea. Don't underestimate the value of good code to make faster progress, even when it doesn't look like it at first glance. When in doubt, remember the famous phrase:[2]

> *Always code as if the person who ends up maintaining your code will be a violent psychopath who knows where you live.*

> —John Woods

9.1 But What Does It Mean to Have a "Good" Code?

If you ever spend more than a couple of minutes talking to a developer, you've probably heard them complaining about a code not being good. If you were present during a debug session, you can hear the angry words, see

---

[1] In the book *Frontend Architecture for Design Systems* by Micah Godbolt: https://fdly.li/09-04.

[2] There is a discussion about who said this phrase, and the final answer was John Wood: https://fdly.li/09-01

the gaze of desperation, or see them leaving the computer in frustration. Sometimes, they decide to check to see who wrote that horrendous piece of code only to discover—in horror—that it was themselves.

Code quality is a very abstract concept. It is very subjective most times, since each developer has their own preferences. At large-scale projects, it will most likely be the result of a contract that all developers decide to follow, so they can understand each other, even if the contract can have things a single developer disagrees with.

Let's say you decided to learn how to paint. When you start a painting class, they will teach you the basics on brushes, paints, sheets, and so on. As you get more and more experienced, you will start to learn complex concepts that not necessarily have to do with the materials and tools, but with art. It's a similar difference between learning a programming language and learning to develop a good code and becoming a great developer. In fact, some of the most important books for developers aren't focused on a programming language, but on these abstract concepts of good and clean code.[3]

Let's take a look at some of the characteristics that can make a code to be good.

9.2 Naming Is Everything!

You decided you want to share a coupon for users from the JollyFarm to use. However, the coupon is only available for purchases that are bigger than a minimum value of $10. The development team added the following logic:

```python
1    # Python
2    if a > 10:
3        c = a - b
```

---

[3] Some examples are from *Clean Code* by Robert Martin and *The Pragmatic Programmer* by David Thomas and Andrew Hunt.

```
4    else:
5       c = a
```

You are probably thinking: What is even going on here? What do "a,"
"b," and "c" stand for? How can someone try to change this if they can't
really understand what was going on?

Now spend a few minutes looking at this next piece of code:

```
1    # Python
2    if amount > 10:
3       amount_to_be_paid = amount - discount
4    else:
5       amount_to_be_paid = amount
```

What do you think? You can see that on line 2 there is a verification
to see if the amount is higher than 10, which is the minimum amount a
purchase must have to be eligible for the discount. If it's true (the amount
of purchase is bigger than 10), the amount_to_be_paid will be the amount
minus the discount (discount is applied), else it will be the amount itself
(discount was not applied).

If you pay close attention, you can see that both pieces of code do
exactly the same thing, but one did a better job explaining what was
happening in there. This is a small example of one of the most basic traits
of code quality: good variable names. A clean code allows the developer to
understand what's going on even if there is no clear documentation or if
they don't have any previous experience on what that code do. If you need
to change the logic, which one would you prefer to work with?

Let's see one more example. Imagine that you are looking at the code
that handles orders. Inside each order, we have a variable called paid.
What do you expect this variable to contain?

- The amount that was paid?

- When the payment was processed?

- If the order was paid or not?

It's kind of impossible to know just by that name. It could be any of the preceding options. Now let's say we change the variable name from `paid` to `is_paid`. What do you expect now? The only answer to the question `is_paid` is yes or no. You don't think of anything else. There is no doubt on what should be there.

What if I change it to `paid_at`? What do you think this refers to? You immediately think of a date. It seems logical that this variable keeps something related to a moment in time when the order was paid. With two simple additional (and small) words, we could make a variable name way easier to work with than before.

Any fool can write code that a computer can understand. Good programmers write code that humans can understand.

—Martin Fowler

It seems simple, but this is the kind of thing that demands thinking. Giving good names for things is considered one of the two most complicated problems in computer science.[4] The examples I gave you were quite straightforward, but there are some complicated things out there. Never underestimate how hard it is to find good names.

---

[4] From the quote "There are only two hard things in Computer Science: cache invalidation and naming things": `https://fdly.li/09-02`

9.3 Software Is Made of Small Pieces

Imagine now that we added the discount logic to the system we saw in the previous section. Then you realize that you want to give bigger discounts for bigger purchases. What to do? We can copy this piece of code, change the values, and use it where we need it. Great! All good, right?

Now imagine that a couple of weeks later, we realize that we better add some expiration dates, or the discounts can be used forever! Because the logic is spread into different places, we have to remember to go into two (or more) places and change it!

The best practice in this case is to encapsulate the code in a single place that can be called every time we need it. To do that, we can use functions. A function is basically something that receives inputs, works with them internally, and returns an output.

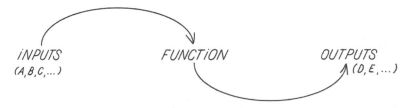

Figure 9-1. *A function is something that receives inputs, works with them, and returns an output*

We can create a function called `calculate_discount` that receives four inputs: the amount a user is buying (`amount`), the discount amount to be applied (`discount_amount`), the minimum amount of a sale required to apply the discount (`minimum_discount`), and the expiration date for the coupon (`expiration_date`).

First, the function needs to check if the coupon is still valid. To do so, it can actually call another function called `is_expired`, and if that function returns `True`, it will just return the original amount, as we won't apply an expired coupon.

Here's the example of how this function would look like:

```python
1   # Python
2   def calculate_discount(amount, discount_amount, minimum_
    amount, expiration_date):
3     if is_expired(expiration_date):
4       return amount
5
6     if amount > minimum_amount:
7       amount_to_be_paid = amount - discount_amount
8     else:
9       amount_to_be_paid = amount
10
11    return amount_to_be_paid
```

This means that every time we need to calculate a discount, we could do something like this:

```python
1   # This will return 18
2   calculate_discount(
3     amount=20,
4     discount_amount=2,
5     minimum_amount=10,
6     expiration_date='2041-09-18'
7   )
```

Now we have a function that we can call every time we need to apply discounts! With this function, we don't need to duplicate code anymore. And if we want to change the criteria for a discount we only need to change one—and only one—place.

This idea can be extrapolated to bigger parts of the codebase. When things are well done, the pieces are well defined and small enough to do a job but not too big that becomes confusing.

> <u>Modularity</u> is how the system is divided into small pieces with clear boundaries, making it easy to maintain and test.

9.4 A Second Pair of Eyes: The Importance of Code Review

<u>Code review</u> (sometimes called peer review) is the review process before we have new code merged into the main codebase. Before being merged into the codebase, it will be reviewed by someone else. This creates an opportunity for developers to learn from each other, improve the quality of code, and share knowledge about the codebase. This is usually made by blocking any new code to be merged until it has express approval by another developer.

A research[5] with over 800 developers found out that finding defects, code improvement, and finding alternative solutions to problems were the top three reasons why developers do and request code review from their peers. But many other important reasons are stated such as share code ownership and team awareness.

---

[5] https://fdly.li/09-03

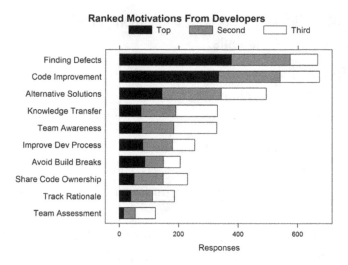

Figure 9-2. *Developers' motivations for code review. Extracted from "Expectations, Outcomes and Challenges of Modern Code Review."* Source: `https://fdly.li/09-03`

Imagine that you are working for weeks on a part of the codebase that other developers on your team aren't familiar with. By asking someone else to review this new piece of code you are introducing, the reviewer is gaining a bit more experience on that area (where they aren't directly working on) and at the same time making sure that you are following all the good standards. Win-win scenario!

In general, the code review involves the following steps:

1.   The author creates a change and submits it for code review.

2.   The reviewers can see the changes that are being proposed to the codebase.

3.   Both developers can start a threaded discussion on specific lines of code.

4.   The author can propose modifications to address reviewers' comments.

5.   This feedback cycle continues until everybody is satisfied or the change is discarded.

It may seem complicated, but code reviews shouldn't be a burden. It should be a lightweight and flexible process. Developers can discuss what's best *for the code* and sometimes compromise when they disagree with each other.

Also, the team should know when to make sure code quality is up to the standards and when we can bend the rules a bit. I have a great example where there was a bug in production and my fix was making the code harder to understand. For me to do the right thing, I would need time, but fixing the bug was time sensitive, as some users were suffering from the problem. The reviewer and I agreed that my code would be merged as it was, but as the bug was fixed, I would work on improving the overall structure of this part of the codebase as a fast-follow task.

If done correctly, this sharing culture can also create an environment where nobody thinks they are above criticism. Even if the person who is reviewing the code is less experienced than the person that wrote it, it's still a valid learning experience. In healthy environments, even the most inexperienced developers can comment, ask questions, and suggest improvements.

9.5 Versioning

Let's say you are working on a dissertation for your masters. You think the document is ready, and you send it to your professor. She comes back with several suggestions. Afraid of losing your changes, you make a copy with a new name, make changes to it, and send the updated document. This cycle goes on and on until you have so many copies you are completely lost. There are so many documents, and every one of them contained changes in different places that it becomes impossible to go back to previous versions. And you are the only person changing this document!

When you have a team of developers working on the same codebase, it's tricky to know what is going on. Some companies work with hundreds or maybe thousands of developers. How can all of this be coordinated? The way this problem was solved was with proper tools for *versioning* the codebase.

Git is the main tool used for software version control in the world. It makes tracking code changes much more simpler, in a way you can trace back to *who* did *what* and *when*. After its launch, in 2005, Git quickly became the default tool, which is used by many companies as the default way of dealing with code.

One fundamental aspect of Git is that every change is packaged and receives an ID that is unique, called a commit. The commit, once added to the pile, becomes part of the history of that code, one you can look back and see when that commit was created and who wrote it.

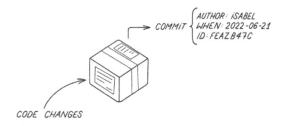

Figure 9-3. *Git allows you to add code changes into a "package" call commit, where you can quickly see who wrote that code and when*

The commits are added to the codebase by many developers, and if, for any reason, someone merged a faulty code, you can identify the last package that was fully working. Then you can remove the faulty commit quickly, returning the system to a stable situation.

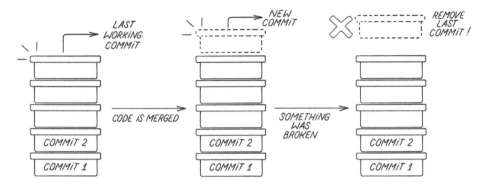

Figure 9-4. *A pile of commits allows us to quickly revert to a previous stable version if a commit containing a bad code is added by accident*

It can also help developers deal with changes being made in the same file, which can also happen even if we try not to do so!

Git is an invaluable tool for developing, and all the main tech companies use it as the default tool for building software in cooperation.

9.6 Documentation

Code, and especially good code, is a great source of written material. However, most projects are so big and complex that code—by itself—isn't enough to enable teams to continue working and improving these systems. The *only* way to properly create these massive projects is through *good* and thoughtful documentation. Documentation can be a dreadful topic, and more often than not, it's the first thing to go out of the window if time is short. However, a lack of documentation is one of the pain points that can make teams go slow, especially when most of the team is lacking context because they are new.

There are different types of documentation, from very technical (mixed in the code) to very high level (for people that have little context to the project). There are also different types of audience as you can have internal documentation that helps developers and teams to work with the project and external documentation that focuses on showcasing how system works to the potential users of that system.

9.6.1 Documentation at Code Level

As you've seen all through this chapter, good variable names, small and well-named functions, etc., are part of developing code that helps people to easily understand what's going on. When we say we should worry about these things, the idea is to create code that is so good that anything explaining it is a redundancy. Here is an example of an unnecessary piece of code documentation:

```
1    # Total amount of the order is the
2    # quantity of each item multiplied by its amount
3    total = quantity * amount
```

Since it's pretty obvious by the names of the variables, the comment becomes unnecessary, even annoying as you spend more time reading the comment than it would take to understand the code. This is true in the majority of cases when code is good, but not all.

There's a common saying that goes[6]

Code is its own best documentation.

—Steve McConnell

This particular phrase is used by some developers that the code is *so good* that no comment should ever be written. You can find people fighting code comments as if they are the plague! However, this phrase is out of context and the complete phrase is

---

[6] In the book *Code Complete* 2nd edition.

Code is its own best documentation. If the code is bad enough to require extensive comments, try first to improve the code so that it doesn't need extensive comments.

—Steve McConnell

The author is very clear: you can't ignore the importance of documenting pieces of code that are hard to understand. You need to try your best to avoid them, or make them as small and concise as possible, but they should exist where they matter.

I know from experience that there are moments where the code needs to do a weird turn that might not be clear at first glance to an unfamiliar person. Maybe the business logic changed for a specific case, maybe it is a temporary hack, it doesn't matter. *This doesn't mean that the developer who wrote that code is not trying their best*, but sometimes complexities happen and you can't avoid them. In these cases, a descriptive code comment can do wonders for the next person reading it and save a lot of time and headaches, as they can quickly understand what happened and why the person who wrote that code did what they did.

9.6.2 Documentation at Development Level

Instructions

One big part of programming is to avoid repeating yourself. A lot of software have the goal to automatize things, but there are several things that either can't or won't be automatized, and you need to describe them somewhere. Which instructions should a new developer follow to set up their environment of work? Which steps should someone do to create that report file? How can someone manually test something they are working with?

The truth is that our memory is highly fallible, and no one should rely on it. One time, I was responsible for a massive system change. It required to exchange some security keys with an external partner. The person in my team who did this the first time never wrote anything down, because they were certain that they would only need to do this once. The problem, as usual, is that things change *all the time*. Because there was no documentation on how to do it, I had to remove them from the priority project they were working on to help me. Not only that, they had to remember everything they did two years ago.

We sat down together, and while they were doing the job, I was writing down what they did, step by step. I also thought what I was doing was useless. If we thought we only needed this once, twice was already enough, and we would never need this again, right? Wrong! A couple of years later, another developer told me she was using the documentation I wrote! Nobody ever expected that the keys would be changed *again*, but thankfully this time they knew exactly what needed to be done!

Documentation saves everyone's time!

Architectural Overviews

As systems become more and more complex, the overall architecture becomes difficult to understand just by reading the code. Complex systems require at least some documentation on how it all works together.

Documentation at an architectural level also helps sharing knowledge between the organization, making sure that all decisions and trade-offs consider the whole scenario and not isolated parts.

Decision Logs

Every day, we need to make decisions big and small. Over time, these decisions pile up, and when we look back, we can't piece them together. We look at something that was decided long ago and scratch our head thinking "why would anyone ever decide on this over that?".

In a team I worked with, we created a decision log where we would log the decision, the trade-offs considered, and who was involved in the decision. This made it easier for us to look back at what happened and asked the involved people more context if that was needed. It also forced conversation between parts as we can't add a decision log without at least some things being written down.

9.6.3 Documentation at a User Level

Eventually, people will start to use the product and interact with it. Some systems are very much intuitive. Social networks, for instance, have very little documentation, and still everyone knows how to use them (most of the time). Other software tend to have more documentation to external users. It's easy to overlook and think that a great product, by itself, can be enough for having users fascinated by it. However, complex products require amazing documentation, and it should be viewed as an important part of the development process—as fundamental as any other features.

There is also the problem that documentation should be always up to date, especially if the system is highly complex. For those systems, undocumented features are the same thing as nonexisting features, because there is no way a user can discover them.

There are basically four different types of documentation that you can and should create for a product:

- **Tutorials**: Learning-based documentation where you take the reader by the hand through a series of steps to complete a project. Mainly focused on new users and/ or beginners. The main purpose is to give the user the best possible start by giving them confidence.

- **How-to guides**: These are problem-oriented guides that take the reader through steps required to solve a common problem. These will turn the learner into a proper user of the software.

- **Background material**: These are documents that will explain why things are the way they are, design decisions, historical reasons, and so on.

- **Reference materials**: These documentations will describe the characteristics and attributes of the product. You can think of them as the "wikipedia" equivalent of products and features.

One thing you should always keep in mind is that documentation is a dynamic thing and, as your software product, should receive feedback from users, should be considered into the development flow, and should improve over time.

9.7 Maintainability at JollyFarm

We want JollyFarm to be successful, and we need to think about it as we are starting our MVP. We start by implementing some guidelines:

- Our developers will work using Git as the versioning system.

- Whenever we change a behavior of the system, we always write the decision and who was involved in it.

- Every code should be reviewed before being merged in production, no matter how urgent and critical it is.

- When scoping a new feature to the ecommerce time should be allocated to think about user documentation.

- The code will follow one single style guideline.

- There is an automated tool to check if all guidelines are followed and forbid code that isn't up to the standards.

All of these can *help* our team and software be in a better place, but it can't *guarantee* quality. We need everyone to think and push toward a better codebase. This can't be a single-person job, it's a team effort. And to fully get to a good maintainable codebase, there is still one piece of the puzzle missing: tests.

9.8 Chapter Summary

Software projects are ever evolving. Being able to easily do this is a fundamental part of building good projects that scale with its success. This is what's called *maintainability*, and although it's not something users can see, it can have a huge impact on how we can work with this system in the future. Some of the things we can do to improve the maintainability of our system:

- Making sure the code has descriptive words that make sense to that context.

- The code is separated into smaller pieces with clear boundaries.

- The code that is introduced is reviewed by other developers so it can be collectively verified and improved.

- All developers in the same project use the same code style, regardless if that's not their preferred way.

- The code uses a tool for versioning in order to know who did what and when. This allows developers to quickly roll back to a previous working version of the software if something goes wrong.

- Good code is good, but great projects have extensive documentation to help everyone get up to speed quicker.

- Documentation is a fundamental part of the job, both internally (other developers and teams) and externally (users). It should be considered part of the job just as much as writing code.

9.9 Further Reading

The Nature of Software Development by Ron Jeffries was a great and easy read to understand good processes to develop software: `https://fdly.li/the-nature`.

Martin Fowler's article is reference in software development, and his article "Is High Quality Software Worth the Cost?" is an amazing post: `https://fdly.li/09-06`.

I absolutely loved Daniele Procida's "What nobody tells you about documentation" where they explained the four types of technical user-facing documentation I used in this chapter (`https://fdly.li/09-78`), and the book *Docs for Developers* focuses on giving practical guidelines to anyone that wants to create great documentation: `https://fdly.li/09-08`.

Still on documentation, I would recommend the great checklist on how to create great user-facing documentation created by Amanda Savluchinske: `https://fdly.li/09-09`.

CHAPTER 10

Guaranteeing Software Quality

End users don't care how your code is implemented; they only care whether your code works.

—David Peter

In the previous chapter, we discussed several topics that can impact the quality of the code and overall productivity of developers writing it. Although all of them are fundamental, there's still a big piece missing: checking that the code does what's intended. At the end of the day, the user doesn't care if your code is perfect. If it doesn't work, it doesn't matter. Beyond the code quality, we also need to be sure, as much as we can, that the code actually works, and the way we do this is by testing.

> *Code without tests is bad code. It doesn't matter how well written it is. Without them, we really don't know if our code is getting better or worse.*
>
> —Michael C. Feathers

© Leticia Portella 2023
L. Portella, *A Friendly Guide to Software Development*,
https://doi.org/10.1007/978-1-4842-8969-3_10

10.1 What Does It Mean to Test a Software?

In Section 9.3, we discussed that when the code is well implemented, you can think of it as a bunch of small functions that work together. One of the reasons is that modularity makes things easier for testing.

Let's take a simplified version of the `calculate_discount` example we saw before:

```python
1   # Python
2   def calculate_discount(amount, discount_amount, minimum_
    amount):
3     if amount > minimum_amount:
4       amount_to_be_paid = amount - discount_amount
5     else:
6       amount_to_be_paid = amount
7
8     return amount_to_be_paid
```

There are two possible results for this function: it either applies the discount or it doesn't. Since we know what is expected of this function, we can use this knowledge to test the behavior.

We can start by testing that when I send an amount that is larger than the minimum amount, the discount is applied. In Python, we could test it by doing this:

```python
1   # Python
2   assert calculate_discount(amount=20, discount_amount=5,
    minimum_amount=10) == 15
```

This code **assert**s that when **calculate_discount** receives the **amount** equal to **20**, the **discount_amount** equal to **5**, and the **minimum_amount** equal to **10**, it will return the same result (==[1]) as **15**.

This test will check if the function is doing as expected, and if it is not, it will raise a warning saying "wait a second, I expected something but got something else!", like you can see in Figure 10-1.

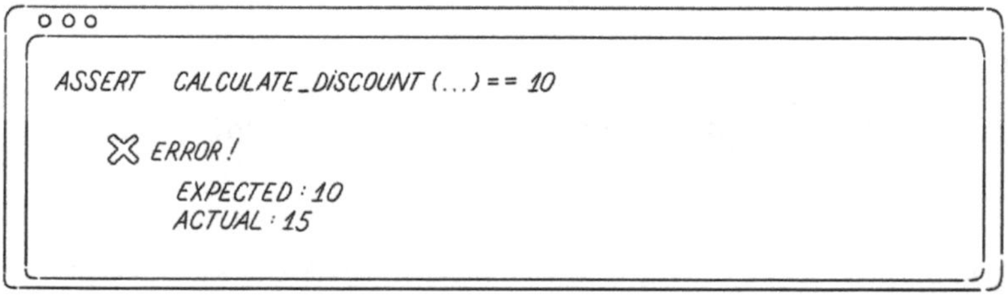

Figure 10-1. *In tests, we can check if what a function does matches our expectations, and if it doesn't, the system returns an error saying that something is wrong*

Since functions are the smallest working part of a software, the tests we create for them are called <u>unit tests</u>. This is because they are checking the smallest unit of code (function) and not the system as a whole. We are not testing, for instance, if this is the function that is called when the user adds a discount to a purchase. We only tested that, if the system calls this function, it will work properly.

The goal of unit testing is to isolate each part of the program and show that each individual part is correct.

---

[1] In most programming languages, a single sign of equal is used to store values, while two (and sometimes three) equal signs are used to verify if two values are the same, such as the example.

10.2 Is There Anything Else?

Now we have a test for the `calculate_discount`. Does this mean we've done our job? Can we say we tested this function?

Well, we can't. We just checked one possible outcome for the function, but we didn't guarantee that if the amount is small, the discount won't be applied. So we can add another test like this:

```python
# Python
assert calculate_discount(amount=9, discount_amount=5,
minimum_amount=10) == 9
```

All good! Is there anything else we need to test? Let's consider one additional scenario: what would happen if we have a discount that is bigger than the original amount. What would happen in the following case?

```python
# Python
calculate_discount(amount=10, discount_amount=15, minimum_
amount=5)
```

If we use the original code, we can see that the result for this function is **-5**, which makes no sense in this context! We can't really have a purchase order with negative amounts! What we would need to do is change the function to handle this behavior. We can guarantee that the amounts are always positive, or in a more extreme case, we can stop the program and raise an error if we end up with a negative amount.

To properly test something, we need to check assumptions and behaviors, looking for all possible outcomes. In fact, what we are looking for are errors: Did we miss something when we were implementing this piece of functionality?

Testing is the process of executing a program with the intent of finding errors.

Even if we expect that we won't ever get to a scenario where this could happen, we need to make sure the system knows how to handle edge cases. There's a nice proverb to live by in software development:[2]

Trust, but verify.

—Russian proverb

10.3 Beyond Unit Tests

In the small example we've seen, we are only testing the behavior of that particular function. It doesn't guarantee the user is actually able to create an order with a discount when they try to do so. The unit test just guarantees one small part of the system works, but there are many, many more aspects to it.

Unit tests are the first step on a ladder of tests that will form a <u>test suite</u>. After we add unit tests, we should add <u>integration</u> tests. Integration tests aim to test how multiple functions work together. While unit tests check if the function works correctly, integration tests check if they are called when they should be.

Finally, we can add *end-to-end* (also known as <u>e2e</u>) tests to make sure that the user experience from start to finish is the one we expect. This means that we will try to reproduce, as best as possible, the user flow through the system: filling forms, clicking buttons and seeing if all pieces of the puzzle are working together.

---

[2] https://fdly.li/10-01

Also, after all this is done, we can still find some value in doing *manual* tests, even after all the other tests were created. Manual tests can act as the last line of defense against bugs.

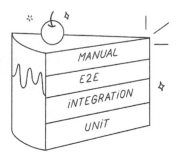

Figure 10-2. *An integrated layer of tests is fundamental to make sure the system works correctly. We can start with unit tests that focus on the behavior of small functions to e2e tests where we reproduce exactly what the user experiences*

One of my teams had a tradition that when we're launching a big new feature, after we test all that we can think of, we gather colleagues and ask them to manually test it. We create long lists of scenarios, but everyone is free to go whatever weird path they want. The idea is to bulletproof the feature, hoping to avoid failures before they go to production. We usually do this at the end of a big feature. A myriad of other tests are written along the way, in the many weeks or months we are working on the project, but the manual tests allow people to go to unexpected places we might not have thought of while building the new feature.

In the case of the preceding example, if we want to do an e2e test, we need to check that the user is able to add a discount coupon to an order, see the discount being applied, and be able to pay the order with the new amount. All parts of the system must work together here: from the web page of adding the discount to the checkout page with the discounted amount and to the payment area.

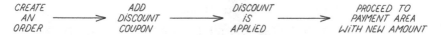

CREATE   ADD   DISCOUNT   PROCEED TO
AN   ⟶   DISCOUNT ⟶   IS   ⟶   PAYMENT AREA
ORDER   COUPON   APPLIED   WITH NEW AMOUNT

Figure 10-3. *End-to-end tests check what the user sees, rather than a specific part of the code*

Each test has its own importance, and the combination of all of them is what helps make a system reliable. Unit tests are amazing, but they are just the first line of defense. If you want to have a working system, a complete and diversified test suite will be your best ally.

10.4 Tests Save Money

In the previous chapter, we discussed how a good software is made of a bunch of small functions working together as clock gears. The problem is that even if you do great work worth of the best clock masters of the world, it doesn't mean it's easy to understand how it all works together. The more complicated the software, the more complicated it is to guarantee that a single change won't break the behavior of something down the line.

Figure 10-4. *Systems always get more and more complex over time, and it's hard to know what parts can be affected by a change, even if the system is well done*

How can you guarantee that if you change one part, others won't start failing? If you have a good test suite, making changes is easier, because you can identify things that were broken before they ever get to production.

Tests should be run often. No code should be added to the codebase if the tests aren't passing. No exceptions.

Let's imagine that you don't have any tests and a user required some new functionality. Changes are made, you manually test the area that you think is involved, and the code is deployed. When the user accesses the system, they realize that something is not working properly. Now there is a cost of having the customer support person to listen and report the error.

After that, a ticket is created and a developer will spend some time debugging to understand the root cause. They spend a couple of hours fixing and then deploying the solution. Finally, your customer support needs to let the user know that the problem is fixed.

There are several tangible costs of dealing with a faulty software, but you also have to consider a cost that you can't really measure: the cost of losing the trust of a customer that is annoyed by your product.

If the system is well tested, the developer can avoid the error and all these costs by catching it in a failing test. Before the code ever get to production, the developer could figure out what is wrong, and the test will help point out where the error is. And the best part: Your customer does not see the error and continues to trust in your company. Who can put a price on the confidence of a customer?

10.5 Tests Also Increase Code Quality

There is one more thing that tests do:[3]

> *By writing tests, developers tend to write code that is more easily testable. The act of designing the tests make developers rethink the design of the code itself: clean, simple code is testable code. If a developer finds that units are hard to test, it provides a good reason and opportunity to simplify those units.*

Bad code is usually hard to test. If we create a culture of testing, the code must be written in a way that is easy to test. Just the act of writing tests can lead to better code!

10.6 When to Test?

The best, ideal scenario is that the tests are added alongside the code. Every new change should be accompanied by tests that guarantee their behavior. This way, your test coverage grows with the complexity of the codebase.

One way to assure tests are being added is to implement some additional verification that checks if every code change is accompanied by a test file or if the new code introduced is being covered by some tests. Code reviewers can also help on this, not allowing untested code to be merged.

Adding tests is as much as a cultural behavior as it is a technical pattern.

---

[3] https://fdly.li/10-04

Tests should also be run in your CI pipeline. Whenever someone writes a new code, the changes should be tested along with *all* tests available in the whole codebase. Then, if the tests started to fail when there's a new code, we have one of two things happening: either the new code is breaking something or there was an expected behavior change.

Never merge code that has failing tests. They are failing for a reason!

If it is the first case, amazing! Tests prevented the addition of a problem to the codebase. Yay! If it is the latter, it should be carefully checked. Changing basic assumptions are considerably less common, and changing a test can be masking a problem. Once done, tests shouldn't be changed, except in highly special cases.

10.7 Tests As the Driver of Development

There's an interesting methodology called test-driven development (TDD) that stimulates developers to write a test *before* ever writing code. A typical TDD implementation works as follows:

1. Define a small function that needs to be implemented.

2. Write a test for such function.

3. Run the test. It should fail since there is no functionality yet.

4. Write the function and check if the tests passed.

5. If the tests didn't pass, refactor the functionality until they do.

6. If the tests did pass, start over with a new functionality.

This way, you can start the code development focusing on what the code *should* do, instead of *how* to do it. If you don't have enough context to write the test, you shouldn't write any code until you do. TDD helps focusing on what's important.

In fact, TDD is also the best methodology for finding and correcting bugs. Whenever a new bug is reported, the first thing to do is to write a test that fails due to that bug. The idea is that you first write a test that fails because that bug exists. Only after you can add the code that will fix the issue (and make the test pass). This way, by the end of it you have a test that guarantees that this bug won't happen again while having full certainty that the fix is actually fixing the bug.

10.8 Testing Performance

So far, we discussed tests that are focused on validation: "Does the code do what it is supposed to do?", but there are many other things that can and should be tested.

For instance, one common problem is a software being broken due to a massive number of users accessing the website at the same time. All of us have been in a situation where we were constantly refreshing a website trying to buy that ticket for that concert we couldn't miss, right?

What we can do is to stress the software by making thousands of requests per second, simulating that your system is crowded, and see how it behaves. This is called a load test. The system will break at some point, but the goal is to identify if the load that the system can handle is enough for how you expect your load to be. If it's not, it's time to add efforts in making the system have more capacity.

Let's take an example. Imagine that you are doing a system that helps people to fill their annual income taxes. Most users will spend most of the year not accessing your system, but then when the deadline approaches, they will all come back to your software!

Contrary to unit tests and integration tests, load tests shouldn't be run as often. They should be carefully planned and executed, and every team should be aware that they will happen.

Another test that can be done is how fast the system can respond, also known as latency test. You can test if a single user creates one order, or ten, or a thousand, and so on. These tests can be highly relevant depending on how much your users are sensible to the response time. Amazon, for instance, has a very low tolerance for low requests.[4] The reason is that the customers that have more data will have the slowest requests. However, they are the customers that are making a lot of purchases, so they are the most valuable ones.

These are just some examples. There are many more out there that can be used in many different ways.

10.9 JollyFarm Is Launched!

After weeks of implementation, the JollyFarm MVP was launched! Because of all of our efforts, we quickly iterated over the requirements, dividing the work into sprints and building up a working software. The test suite we built helped us deliver a good system that works well. Farmers are selling like never before, and customers are very impressed with the quality of the product! Now people are relying on your software to do their business. We can't afford to not be available, right? It's time to start thinking about what can go wrong!

---

[4] In *Designing Data-Intensive Applications* by Martin Kleppmann.

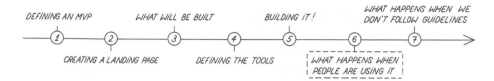

Figure 10-5. *We now have people using our product, and we know what we need to be prepared for*

10.10 Chapter Summary

Testing is one of the most fundamental things that should be done to both guarantee software quality and to make it easier, safer, and cheaper to add new features in the future. The main types of tests are automatized and should be run often, such as

- **Unit tests**: Focused on testing functions, the smallest piece of code you have

- **Integration tests**: Focused on testing the interaction between different parts of the system

- **e2e tests**: Tests that go over a user's path to see if the whole system is behaving as the user expects

There are also additional tests that can be done from time to time, to make sure the system can handle unexpected amounts of customers or data, such as

- **Load test**: Focused on verifying if the system can handle lots of requests at the same moment in time

- **Latency test**: Focused on checking how long the system will take to handle larger amounts of data

Tests are fundamental, and fully testing the system should be as critical as planning a new feature.

10.11 Further Reading

The issue 10 of the *Increment* magazine (https://fdly.li/10-02) has a lot of excellent articles about industry leaders and their culture in testing. You can also find that tests and test infrastructure are also part of many companies when they discuss how they develop code on the issue 3 about development (https://fdly.li/10-03).

The chapter "Automate Tests" from the book *Building Software Teams* by Joost Visser et al. has a good high-level and not too technical overview of the types of tests and what to look out for when building test infrastructures: https://fdly.li/10-04.

The chapter "Testing Overview" from the book *Software Engineering at Google* by Titus Winters, Tom Manshreck, and Hyrum Wright gives a good overview on the practical aspects of testing culture at Google as well as the challenges of having an enormous amount of tests running all the time: https://fdly.li/10-05.

I particularly liked the article "Testing as communication" by Nelson Elhage: https://fdly.li/10-06.

CHAPTER 11

Working 24/7: Making Software Available at All Times

Forget your mistakes but remember what they taught you.

—Vannetta Chapman

Congratulations! JollyFarm is now a successful product, with farms and customers happy and healthy. This is really impressive, and you should be really proud. But now that the product is out there and people are relying on it, we need to think: What will we do if something goes bad? What if the database is unavailable? Or if a human error accidentally causes a big problem?

Errors will happen. You need to both avoid them and be prepared for them.

We need JollyFarm to work correctly even in the face of adversity. We need it to be *reliable*. While maintainability focuses on the quality of software internally, <u>reliability</u> is guaranteeing to the best of our abilities that the system is always available when people want to use it.

The typical expectations of a reliable software are as follows:

- It performs as the user expects.

- It can tolerate users using it in unexpected ways.

- It has a good performance under expected data.

- It prevents any unauthorized access and abuse.

11.1 What Indicates a Reliable System?

The first thing we want to do is make sure JollyFarm will always be available for farmers and customers to use at any time, day or night. To do that, we can measure the percentage of time in which the system is up and running. This is called the system uptime.

Uptime is measured in terms of the number of 9s. The higher the number of 9s, the more reliable is the system. When we say a system has five 9s of uptime, we are saying that the system is available 99.999% of the time. This means that in a year the system can't be unavailable for more than 5.26 minutes!

Availability	%	Downtime per Year
One 9	90%	36.53 days
Two 9s	99%	3.65 days
Three 9s	99.9%	8.77 hours
Four 9s	99.99%	52.60 minutes
Five 9s	99.999%	5.26 minutes

Another important metric to evaluate how well a system is performing is latency, which is the time it takes for one request to go all the way to the server, be processed, and back. Latency is a highly variable metric, and it depends on a lot of things such as the computer capacity and physical distance between the client and the server. Because of that, instead of using latency as a fixed number, we also treat it in terms of percentile.

Let's take the past requests of JollyFarm and check how long it takes for the system to return a response. Take a look at Figure 11-1 and think if we can properly say that the latency is 118 milliseconds, the average value of the requests. Do you think this number makes a good representation of JollyFarm's latency?

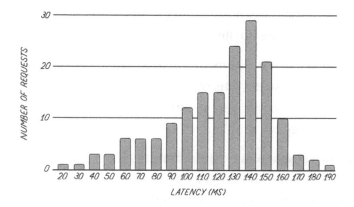

Figure 11-1. *A histogram of latency of a system. The average value (118ms) is not the best to describe how the majority of users are experiencing the system, so typically the values of p95 and p99 are more reliable*

Well, you can see that there are a lot of users that will need to wait more than 118ms for the request. That's why instead of getting the average, we should use the percentile to describe this metric. If we say that in every 100 requests, 95 will be faster or equal to 160ms, we have a number that is much more closer to the reality of Figure 11-1. This is called the p95 metric, and it's a metric we can rely on.

Some companies even prefer to use the p99—which in our case is 180ms—to have an even more real representation of how the majority of their users are experiencing the system.

11.2 Monitoring Is the Basis of Reliable Systems

Latency and uptime are only two examples of a thousand metrics that we can measure to check how healthy the system is. You can check for the number of successful and failed requests, the number of status codes that indicate an unexpected server failure (500s), etc. All these metrics should be available together in dashboards that can be easily accessed and where a developer can quickly see if something went wrong.

Good dashboards are not an easy thing to achieve, they must

- **Be easily comprehensible**: They should be as simple as possible, so anyone, regardless of how much knowledge they have, can understand what's going on and if there is a problem or not.

- **Be in a single place**: Understanding if the system is healthy or not shouldn't be hard. There must be one main area for checking the health of the system. Any complementary information should live in a different place from what's important.

- **Have a clear goal**: If something changes in a dashboard and there is no action to be taken, the dashboard shouldn't exist!

Figure 11-2 is an example of a dashboard of latency. Each bar indicates how long it took for a single request to be processed. The dashed line indicates the upper limit we consider acceptable. We can quickly see that from 10:20 to 10:40 we had a bunch of requests that went beyond what's acceptable.

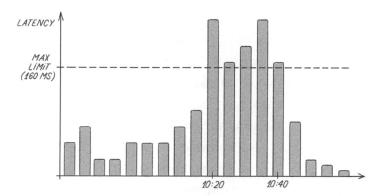

Figure 11-2. *Dashboards are a useful way of quickly identifying how a system is doing and which limit is acceptable for this metric*

Dashboards have another advantage: you can integrate the dashboard with an alarming system that can page an <u>on-call</u> developer to look at the problem. In the preceding example, if the latency becomes too slow (>160ms) for over a limit (say 5 minutes), the alarm can be triggered and someone will be paged to fix the problem.

Imagine that the system has been slow for quite some time. What's worse: knowing this started 10 minutes ago or knowing because your main customer called you in full panic mode? Systems will break, but worse than errors are errors happening without you knowing. Dashboards are the main way of knowing what's wrong, and alerts guarantee someone will investigate why it is going off.

11.3 What Happens When Something Is Wrong

Let's consider the scenario where there is a problem and it's 2am. Laura is the on-call developer of JollyFarm, so she awakes with the paging alarm. She wakes up and gets her computer. Her team agreed that she has 5 minutes to be online and acknowledge the problem (this response time is called the <u>Service Level Agreement (SLA)</u>).

199

Laura's acknowledgment just tells the alarm system that she is aware of the problem and working on it. If Laura wasn't able to answer the alert, there is a predefined hierarchy that the alert will go through. It can call her house phone; if she still doesn't answer, the system will call a secondary developer or the whole team, eventually getting to the team manager or even higher if the alert goes unacknowledged.

In this case, the alert was acknowledged, so no one else was paged. The first thing she needs to do is *triage* the problem: "How bad is it?" She sees the dashboards of the system health, and she notices that something is wrong: all requests are returning a status code 500. Nobody—not farmers nor customers—is able to use the JollyFarm system. Something is definitely broken. This is an incident: a real (and possibly big) problem is happening. She knows that the Jolly Co has a list of incident severity that will help her classify the problem. She takes a look at the list:

- **Severity 3 (Sev-3 or S3)**: Some issue that requires action, but doesn't affect users to use the product. This needs to be solved, but it can wait until working hours to be solved.

- **Severity 2 (Sev-2 or S2)**: A part of users is having some difficulties and may have lost part of functionalities. It might demand some immediate work; it's up to the on-call developer to define what's best.

- **Severity 1 (Sev-1 or S1)**: A good part of users can't use a significant part of the system.

- **Severity 0 (Sev-0 or S0)**: There is a severe impact that affects the majority of users. It might put the whole company in risk and might demand leadership involvement and require external communication.

She looks at the dashboards, and she quickly realizes that this problem is causing problems to every one trying to use the JollyFarm app, and none of them is able to do anything. This is clearly an S0. Because it is so critical, she also paged the communication team, so they can share an official communication to their users.

She starts to investigate, and it looks like the issue is coming from something that she is not familiar with. This may be caused by some infrastructure maintenance that she knows was happening earlier that day. She pages that team so they join her in trying to figure out what's happening.

Both she and the on-call developer from the other team (and any other developer that was paged as well) form a <u>war room</u> as they need quick communication with each other.

They create a hypothesis for what could be happening, investigate if that theory is true, and report back to everyone involved.

One of the developers in the room is responsible for *coordinating* the situation, called the incident manager. This person will not be responsible for fixing the problem, but managing expectations. They will be responsible for making sure the communication team is making the company's announcement so the customers know what's going on. They also need to make sure to wake up the legal team to review contracts and make sure what agreements this outage is breaking and what needs to be done. They also take notes regarding the development of the incident for later.

Now that everyone is on top of the problem, the goal is to *mitigate* the problem. This doesn't mean to, necessarily, discover the problem that caused the page. It's 2am and everybody should be asleep. The developers should focus on returning the system back to a stable situation, to stop the bleeding. They should let people with rested brains during normal work hours to deal with finding *why* the problem happened. If they also find the why while fixing the problem, great! But this is not the priority here.

Once the system is back to normal and the situation is stable, everyone can go back to sleep. On the next day, the incident is not over yet. As important as fixing the problem is to make sure it won't happen *again*. We need to write a <u>postmortem</u>. Postmortems are documents that detail the who, what, where, when, and why of incidents after they occur. It will typically have

- A short description of the incident

- An evaluation of its severity and impact

- The timeline of the incident

- An account of how it was triaged and mitigated

- What went well during the incident response

- What went poorly during the incident response

- Follow-up tasks that need to be addressed so this incident isn't repeated

The most important thing about postmortems is that they are **not**, in any way, a witch hunt. Good postmortems are blameless and/or don't even have the name of the developers even if the whole thing was caused by one.

Any report after an incident should be blameless and, ideally, not even have the name of the people involved in it. The goal is avoiding this problem to be repeated, not blame individuals.

Some companies consider that the incident is over when the system is back to normal, while others require all the follow-up tasks to be finished to fully consider an incident over.

As you can now imagine, on-call is a difficult and stressful process. This is especially true if you are a new developer on the team. There should be a procedure to add new people to on-call rotation due to the fact that the developer might need to work alone in the middle of the night, without the support of their peers. Some teams require a certain number of months, a specific training, or even a scheme of shadow rotation, where a new member follows an older member during a real on-call rotation.

11.4 What Can Go Wrong?

11.4.1 Hardware Faults

We know that a server can run in *any* computer, but *should* it run in any computer? The answer is no. The reason is that not every computer is reliable, so you shouldn't trust your product (and company) to any computer out there.

A computer requires a lot of things to work properly: it needs energy, access to the Internet, a fast CPU, working cables, cool temperatures, and so on. If you are selling to the whole world, you want people to be able to access your software even if you are currently in a blackout and can't do anything about it!

Hardware fault is usually the most common adversity you can probably think of and one of the most complicated ones to handle. A computer in your bedroom can work, but it's not even close to an ideal scenario when we are talking about real companies. One option is to build a <u>data center</u>, a room specialized to store a lot of computers, with good access to the Internet, a backup generator, strong air conditioning, etc.

To build a data center, you need to make some perspectives of how many users and requests you expect, so you can buy enough computers for your current and future reality. You also need to hire a couple of dedicated personnel to handle the complexity of this system and guarantee that it is all working well and to quickly fix what isn't.

You can imagine how expensive building and scaling a data center can get. That's why, in most cases, companies prefer to use the infrastructure provided by other companies through renting their data centers. Anytime you run a software in another company's computer, we say you are working "in the cloud." The companies that provide these types of services are called hosting providers, and there are many examples of them, from big techs to local companies.

Hosting providers guarantee some reliability standards such as connection with a secure and stable Internet, electric power with spare generators, etc. They also provide some additional software services that when one computer fails, others will be available, and your software can be automatically redirected to the new machine.

Imagine that you went and decided to build the data center in your office. You made a calculation of how many clients and requests per second you expect, and this data center should handle. Amazing. You invested money and time, and after a couple of months, it's ready to go. Then your business is a huge hit! You are getting many more clients than you ever imagined! What happens to your data center? Unless you can build new infrastructure quicker than getting new clients, the system will not handle as many requests, and it will go down.

Cloud infrastructure allows you to grow and add more computer resources as you need or reduce them if you are not using any. This is a small part of making your software scalable, and scalability is also an important part of any system.

Scalability is the capacity of a system to handle a growing usage without failing or lowering performance.

Many of these hosting providers also allow you to only pay as you use them. Let's say that you have a single computer handling all the requests. You pay for that computer. Then, as you start receiving more and more requests, you can automatically add a second or even a third machine to handle this! Later, when there are fewer requests, you can remove these additional machines and just stay with a single one. You will have to pay for the extra machines, but only when you are using it. This *pay-as-you-go* feature is extremely attractive, since computers (especially powerful ones) are always expensive.

Finally, there is another advantage of using cloud infrastructure for your application. Although you might think that the Internet is as fast as instantaneous, the reality is that geographic distance impacts the speed of requests. For instance, a request from Tokyo to Paris can take more than 230 milliseconds.[1] It seems fast, but if you take that each request has at least two ways (from a client to a server and back), we are talking about 0.5 seconds for a single request just to move from one side to the other (without the time it will take for the server to process it). If you ever got angry with a website that took forever to load, you can imagine how happy your Parisian clients will be if the server is in Tokyo. On the other hand, a request from Paris to London takes about 8 milliseconds. If the majority of your clients are in Paris, using a data center in London will be a much better decision than one in Tokyo.

You can leverage the locations of hosting providers to choose the location that works best for your clients, even if they are not in your country. That's why the default way of doing software today is using rented hardware infrastructure, instead of building anything. Unless there is a specific need for you to build a data center, using cloud infrastructure is the best and cheapest way to handle hardware reliability.

---

[1] https://fdly.li/11-01

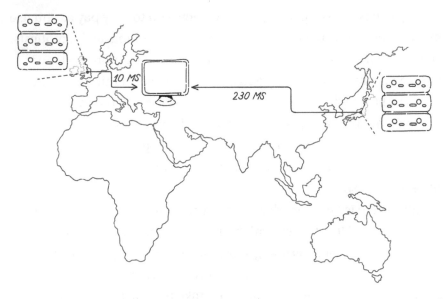

Figure 11-3. *Whenever we talk about hardware, we need to consider physical distance. The farther away your server is from your clients, the longer they will need to wait for a request to go all the way to the server and back*

11.4.2 Software Errors

The same way a hardware can fail, the JollyFarm software can—and probably will—fail at some point. And as we've seen before, its software will also use other software systems, and those software systems can fail as well.

If you were alive in the turn of the millennium, you will probably remember the Millennium bug (also known as Y2K). Most programs at the time used to represent years with only two digits (assuming the first two were 19). Because of that limitation, at the turn of the millennium programs wouldn't be able to differentiate the year 1900 from the 2000. If this happened, the programs could generate corrupted data, suffer malfunction, or even shut down entirely, leaving billions of damage in its path. Thankfully, the authorities listened to specialists, and estimates put the cost of fixing this bug in the order of $100 billion in the United States alone.[2]

Other software errors can come from complex scenarios that can create a combination that wasn't fully tested and addressed while developing a feature. The more complex the scenarios, the easier it is to introduce a combination that is unexpected and can cause trouble later on. We can test our software well enough, but one time or another, an edge case can slip by, and then you have to deal with a bug in production!

Software failures can come from changes in the way we expect the program to behave or bugs introduced in production.

11.4.3 Human Errors

If things like hardware and software can fail, what can we say about humans? Similarly to other failures, human errors should be considered and minimized same as any other. There are countless possible causes for defects caused by human errors: an unpredicted scenario, a typo, a wrong command typed in the wrong place, and so on.

There is a famous incident caused by a human error where an engineer accidentally deleted a database and lost six hours of data from their clients. Almost 300GB of data were compromised, and the incident hit the headlines. When an error like this happens, it's never because of the one person who triggered it. A whole series of things have happened and failed to create a problem this big. The person was just the unfortunate one to trigger it, but not the responsible. Systems and teams should be resilient to single points of failure, especially human ones. *Always.*

---

[2] https://fdly.li/11-02

Case study

To better understand the failures that lead to a catastrophe, let's examine a *very* real scenario:[3]

> *Today was my first day on the job as a Junior Software Developer and was my first non-internship position after university.*
>
> *I was given a document detailing how to setup my local development environment, which involves creating my own personal database from some test data. After running the command, I was supposed to copy [some information] outputted. Unfortunately, instead of copying the values outputted, I used the values the document had.*
>
> *Apparently those values were actually for the production database. Then, the tests [...] clear existing data between test runs which basically cleared all the data from the production database. It wasn't about 30 or so minutes after did someone actually figure out what I did.*
>
> *The [manager] told me to leave and never come back. He also informed me that legal would need to get involved due to severity of the data loss. [...] From what I can tell the backups were not restoring and it seemed like the entire development team was on full panic mode.*

How did a tragedy such as this one happened?

Keep credentials safe

In the 1970s and 1980s, a company's biggest asset was their physical things: computers, machines, and chairs. In the 21st century, the most relevant thing a company has is data: customer data.

---

[3] Original message: `https://fdly.li/11-03`. Thankfully, they got a thousand nice messages calming them down regarding their "mistake."

Would you write down a safe combination on a paper? No! Your production database is equivalent of a safe full of gold. It should have secure and protected credentials, and these credentials should be kept safe. Writing credentials on paper is definitely *not* a safe way of storing them.

Restrict access to changes

Even in the case of someone having credentials, not everyone should be allowed to do everything. A *junior* developer shouldn't be allowed to delete the production database on their own. The system should have different roles for different people. If someone needs to read the data, they can request a read-only access. The system should make it harder for inexperienced people to change things that they might be unknowingly changing.

However, as we've said before, people are prone to errors, and even senior developers can make mistakes. One way of providing a safe net to avoid mistakes is require two sets of authorization for acts that will change production data. This is the same structure of a code review, but at much higher stakes!

Backups are fundamental

Data, once lost, is lost. The way we deal with the possibility of losing data is creating replications. By creating replications, we decrease the likelihood of losing all the data. This is called a backup, and the further away a backup is from the original source, the better. Creating backups of production data is a fundamental part of the process of developing a reliable software system. A working backup system should be as a priority as the system being run. Without backups, you are vulnerable to *any* problem becoming a *gigantic* problem.

Have backups. And always make sure they work.

Errors show a process problem, not a developer problem

Who do you think was responsible for the preceding case? The answer is *no one* and everyone. When a problem of this magnitude happens, it wasn't a single mistake that caused it. It was a series of mistakes and procedure problems that happened in a specific order, culminating into a big problem. A single person, by themselves, shouldn't be allowed enough power to create a problem of this size. There were several safety procedures that failed to allow someone to be the trigger factor.

There is a story[4] that an employee caused a $10 million loss to a company. They enter the CEO office expecting to get fired. The CEO turns and says: "Fire you? I just paid you a $10 million lesson, there is no way I am letting you go."

People are never to blame, processes are.

Test, test, test, test!

Systems should be tested, and procedures should be tested. Is the alerting system working? Are the backups working? Are the developers ready for an incident when they occur? Tests should happen often, and they should be taken seriously.

Some companies take tests to extreme levels. To make sure their systems are always built to be reliable, Netflix created a software called *Chaos Monkey*[5] that randomly creates failure in the company's production services without telling any of the teams. This way, teams can never really know when it is going to happen, and they should think about their systems to be prepared for failures at all times.

---

[4] I couldn't verify the original source for this story.
[5] More on https://fdly.li/11-04

11.5 Some Strategies for Safer Deploys

One of the most critical moments in the software development cycle is when code is being deployed in production. In the vast majority of cases, your system is working well and the deployment is the moment where bugs can be introduced and things can go wrong. Nevertheless, continuous deployment is part of the modern software development, and deploys should happen frequently! There are several strategies that can improve the quality of changes being introduced and help the stream of deployment to happen constantly.

Feature flags

Feature flags are a way of directing users to different system behavior easily. Imagine that you created a new feature in the ecommerce that is still under development. The feature flag can act as a switch; when it's on, users can see the new feature, otherwise they can't.

This way, the developers can continue to safely add code for the new feature with no impact on users until everyone is confident they can flip the switch. You can also make the switch to be user specific. This way, you can allow some users to see the new feature until you are more confident that this new behavior is working and finally flip the switch to everyone.

Since the feature flag is simpler to turn on or off, the change between behavior is much faster than a deploy. This means that if something is wrong, it's much safer to revert if something went poorly.

Metrics, metrics, metrics!

You can't know if a system is healthy if you don't have the metrics to check its health. Metrics are always critical, but at deployment time, they are even more critical. You need to be able to quickly assess if the system had a change in behavior that is causing pain to users. Otherwise, how can you act if you don't know if something's wrong?

Ramping up deploys

Another strategy is to roll out the deploys in small incremental steps, making sure that the system keeps working at all times. The idea is that you start the deploy by sending just a couple of users to a new version of the system. As metrics continue to show the system is stable, you start increasing the percentage of users that are getting the new version until all users are using the new version. This is called a canary release or incremental rollout, and it's highly useful, as you can address a problem before most of your users are suffering.

Automated rollback

Some companies implement a strategy of automated rollback. What happens is that if, at any moment during deployment, the metrics went bad and the system looks unhealthy, the deploy is canceled and everything goes back to the previous (working) version. Of course, all of this is only possible if the whole deployment process and metrics are automatized!

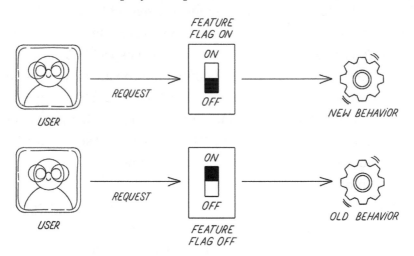

Figure 11-4. *Feature flags are like a light switch you can use to quickly switch between new and old behavior, for a small rollout and quick rollback of new behavior*

11.6 Using Architecture to Prevent Known Points of Failure

When we are dealing with multiple complex systems, there are points of failure that can be expected and thus prevented. The database might be down, the third-party company you rely on is offline, and many other scenarios are unwanted but expected. So we can organize and change our architecture to adapt and be resilient to those failures.

Let's consider that one day the communication with a database is interrupted and the JollyFarm server can't save data to it anymore. This should be an expected error because things can fail and they most certainly will, at one time or another.

We can create an architecture where there is a primary database where everything gets written. In certain periods of time, this primary database copies the data to a secondary database. If the primary database fails, the secondary can assume as primary, and there's *almost* no loss of data nor unavailability.

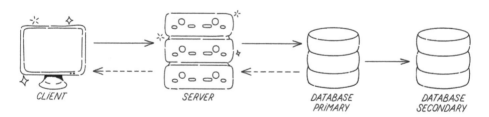

CLIENT   SERVER   DATABASE   DATABASE
                                PRIMARY   SECONDARY

Figure 11-5. *The architecture of a system can help deal with known failures that can happen at anytime. Creating multiple databases that duplicate data is a strategy in case the primary database is down, a secondary database can take over without loss of information*

Part of designing software architecture is also predicting where we expect things to fail and how we can be resilient to them!

11.7 Can We Avoid a Crisis?

Problems can't be avoided, but crisis can be managed. GitLab became an example of what a good crisis management looks like. In January 2017, a developer deleted the production database, the website was completely offline, and 300GB of data was lost.

Instead of trying to hide the massive problem they were facing, GitLab was completely open about it. They communicated openly that this was happening and that they were working on it. Not only that, they opened a shared document where developers were adding notes about the incident in real time. Later, they also started a live transmission with the developers working on the issue. After the incident, they published the postmortem, allowing developers all over the world to learn from the case.

Figure 11-6. *GitLab had a massive incident in 2017, but instead of being remembered by the problem, they became a reference on how to manage a crisis properly*

Eventually, they did lose a total of six hours of data, but this incident is now remembered as an example on how to deal with a crisis the best way possible.

Not all crisis will be this massive, potential-to-ruin-company bad. They can vary from a small bug that really annoys a customer to things like outage of systems and financial loss. The reality is that a crisis—in all its scales—will happen, one way or the other. It's impossible to create systems that are infallible, even if we do our best. We need to empower people to feel safe when it happens and use the crisis as an opportunity to do better. As the amazing Judy Smith, a crisis management specialist, says:

> *There's always an opportunity with crisis. Just as it forces an individual to look inside himself, it forces a company to reexamine its policies and practices.*

> —Judy Smith

That's it! Now you have a full working product and know what to expect when people are using it. It's time for us to take a quick look on what happens when we don't follow the best practices.

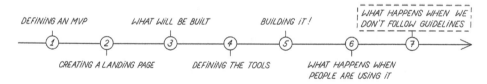

Figure 11-7. *We now have to learn what happens when we don't follow the good guidelines on building software*

11.8 Chapter Summary

We want systems to be available 24/7, but the only way to do that is to think about the system reliability. Errors are unavoidable, but being able to quickly be alerted of failures and recover from them are the things you must worry when thinking about system reliability.

When something goes bad in a software system, we call this an incident and attribute an impact severity on it. After an incident is resolved, a blameless postmortem guarantees that the knowledge gained during this incident is properly shared. The postmortem should also contain the actions to prevent this of ever happening again. As crisis can't be avoided, we must do our best to learn from it.

Some things we can do to avoid problems are as follows:

- Have metrics and dashboards that can quickly tell if something is wrong.

- Identify points of failure and use the system architecture to be resilient to those failures.

- Have procedures in place to make sure the backups and alarming system are always working.

- Have different roles for people and require two people's authorization for critical procedures.

- Use feature flags while building new features to quickly switch between new and old behavior.

- Roll out new code slowly and revert back if metrics start to fail.

11.9 Further Reading

I found the first issue of the *Increment* magazine to be a source for a broad view on industry practices regarding incident management and on-call rotations: https://fdly.li/11-05.

The talk "Critical Incidents: A Guide for Developers" by Laís Varejão was my first contact with the topic of crisis management and was a huge inspiration for this chapter: https://fdly.li/11-06. She also created a checklist on how to deal with critical incidents that you should have at hand at all times: `https://fdly.li/11-07`.

Both the GitLab postmortem about their database outage (`https://fdly.li/11-08`) and the Reddit thread with the incident that we saw in the case study (`https://fdly.li/11-09`) are excellent source of materials to visualize real-case scenarios.

Atlassian has a ton of material on incident management, from roles of people involved in the incident to why and how to communicate with affected customers: `https://fdly.li/11-10`.

The talk "Debugging Under Fire: Keep your Head when Systems have Lost their Mind" by Bryan Cantrill had some interesting points I was not expecting from someone coordinating a massive incident. The author discussed that they needed to prepare for a multiple-day incident and organize things like rounds of sleep, as sleep deprivation is a common problem during massive incidents: `https://fdly.li/11-11`.

CHAPTER 12

The Monster Behind the Door: Technical Debt and Legacy Code

Good programmers know what to write. Great ones know what to rewrite (and reuse).

—Eric S. Raymond

For the past three chapters, we discussed things we can do to make the JollyFarm a good software system, both in the present as well as in the future. Making sure the code is well compartmentalized, the code quality is up to standards, and there is a good test suite wrapping all this. But we all know that one time or the other, things slip. Deadlines are short, resources might be scarce, and corners have to be cut. What do we do then? It's time we discuss what happens when we don't follow the guidelines we discussed throughout this book.

© Leticia Portella 2023
L. Portella, *A Friendly Guide to Software Development*,
https://doi.org/10.1007/978-1-4842-8969-3_12

12.1 Technical Debt

In real life, lending money from someone (creating a debt) allows you to speed up the development of your business. It benefits you but it comes with a cost: you need to pay interest on that money. The only reason why this is a good idea is because you believe that your growth will be bigger than the interest you will pay, so you decide to take the risk. Something similar can happen in software development, and Ward Cunningham created the term <u>technical debt</u> to explain the shortcuts we make while creating software.

Technical debt is the idea that we can take shortcuts while creating code (complicated logic, not following industry standard quality, etc.) that generates a debt (the code becomes hard to maintain). The reason we do this is to move faster even if we are sacrificing some internal quality. With code in production, you can learn more from users, get more investment, and increase revenue.

The problem is that this technical debt also comes with an "interest": it's more expensive to improve something than it is to build it correctly from the start. As with real life, if we leave the debt long enough without repaying it, we can become "bankrupt."

Technical debt is the idea of taking shortcuts in order to move faster. This means we need to go back and fix it, or we can end up in an unmanageable state.

The main problem with technical debt is that it's a silent monster. It's hard to see its impact until it's so big you think you feel like you can't tackle it anymore. As we've discussed in Chapter 9, the worse the code, the harder it is to work with it. The technical debt will eventually slow the product development, and your users will notice it, even if the roots of the problem are far away from them.

The debt doesn't always come because of time constraints. I once was working on this project that had a very complex implementation of a business logic. I spent months trying to understand all the scenarios and corner cases. It was a constant source of pain for our team, and it was very easy to accidentally introduce bugs, as we could hardly understand the whole picture. The code needed refactoring for sure. This debt was not only caused by time constraints to push something out of the door. Our whole understanding of the business logic led us to believe that we needed this complicated logic. As the time passed and we learned more about the business, we were able to come up with a simpler and more elegant solution.

12.2 Technical Debt Is the Same As "Bad Code"?

In 1982, James Q. Wilson and George Kelling introduced the broken windows theory that said:[1]

> *If a window in a building is broken and is left unrepaired, all the rest of the windows will soon be broken. This is as true in nice neighborhoods as in rundown ones. [...] One unrepaired broken window is a signal that no one cares, and so breaking more windows costs nothing.*
>
> —James Q. Wilson and George Kelling

The broken windows theory has become known because of the big implications it had on improving social aspects of urban environments, but it is as valid in software development as it is in cities. If one day a developer introduces a big change without tests, other developers will start to realize that untested behavior is allowed and repeat the pattern. The

---

[1] From Wikipedia's article: `https://fdly.li/12-01`

same is valid to almost all the things we discussed in Chapter 9. Developing and maintaining good code takes as much effort and a good community behavior as maintaining a collective urban environment nice and clean.

Technical debt is a *conscious* decision to not take the best road, while *bad code* is just a broken window left unfixed. Technical debt demands understanding that this was a trade-off, and we need to go back and make things better. Bad code is just showing that we don't care about this code, so we might as well break any other windows we like. Bad code happens when we don't make clear the trade-offs being made, when there is no plan on going back and fixing it. It's just... bad.

12.3 When We Go Bankrupt: Legacy System

There is a type of code that no one likes to change called the legacy system. Legacy systems are, most of all, a difficult thing to work with. This is a fairly broad definition, so let's go to a more formal one:[2]

> *When we refer to a system being legacy what we're really saying is that the system is built in a way that differs from how we'd choose to do so today.*
>
> —Robert Annett

There's also another dimension on legacy code that I particularly like:[3]

> *Legacy code is typically used to describe code that lacks in quality and that we didn't write ourselves.*
>
> —Adam Tornhill

---

[2] From *Working with Legacy Systems* by Robert Annett: https://fdly.li/12-06
[3] From *Prioritizing technical debt as if time and money matters* by Adam Tornhill: https://fdly.li/12-02

This means that legacy systems aren't born from one day to the other. There were several small decisions, small broken windows left unfixed. As time goes they pile up and when you least expect.

These definitions are interesting because they don't necessarily mean that the code was written a *long* time ago. A system that was written poorly a couple of years ago can be as much of a legacy as one written many, many years ago.

The major aspect of a legacy code is that it is *important* to the business. It must have value; otherwise, we could just as easily remove it entirely. So legacy code matters, even if we all have a horrible time dealing with it.

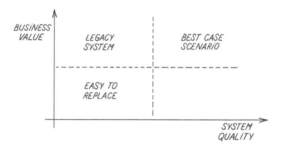

Figure 12-1. *A legacy system is one that has poor quality but has a lot of impact in the business. If a system has poor quality but no real business value, it can be easily replaced or even removed*

12.4 Why Can't We Just Move Away from a Legacy System?

At this point, you might be wondering why we would end up in this situation. Why did we let the system become legacy instead of constantly updating it? It's easy to think you can get out of it, but the truth is a bit more nuanced.

Imagine that you work for a company that has a massive and well-known product. The product is a legacy software that runs on a local data center (instead of the cloud). This data center was an investment made many years ago and cost tons of money to the company. Let's say the main product of the company runs on those computers, and you are eager to move them to something more modern. What are the problems you might face while making the change?

Consider the best-case scenario: you have the buy-in of the leadership. You can start building a replacement software from scratch using new technologies that won't be using the old data center, but the best cloud system that exists. It will take months to rewrite the whole legacy system. In the meantime, your customers are still using the product on the legacy code, bugs will continue to be fixed, and maybe you will still need some new features you promised to big customers.

Now imagine that you completely outdid yourself, and the rewrite is ready way ahead of schedule! Now you have a shiny new product on the state-of-the-art technology. Everyone is excited to get rid of the legacy systems and start prompting your customers to change to this new version of your software. Things are going well, but then one of your biggest clients decided that migrating to the new version is too much of a hassle and they just won't. Congratulations! Now you are stuck with your legacy code, because you can't afford to lose this customer.

In the worst-case scenario, the leadership of the company may not even want to remove the software from the local data center, as it was a big investment that might not be fully paid yet. The local data center is a bit old, their hardware doesn't support newer versions of some of the software you need, and guess what? You are still stuck with the legacy system.

As you can see, it isn't simple to just get rid of legacy systems, and the chances that your company will need to deal with them eventually increase over time.

12.5 When you have to work with a Legacy System

You are happy building the shiny new JollyFarm MVP, which is as far away from a legacy code as it can get. But someone in the Jolly Co sees the good work you are doing in it and ask if you can please also take care of another system that's been around for a while... you know, since you are doing so well...

The dreadful moment comes, and you need to deal with a legacy software. What shall you do? The first thing to do is actually understand specifically why this software is considered a legacy. You know legacy means hard, but it doesn't mean *everything* will be hard. It's time to understand where the struggles are coming from.

Why is this system considered a legacy?

There are several things that can contribute to a software being flagged as legacy: Which ones are affecting this particular system? Is this system running in old hardware that can't bc updated? Was this written in a programming language that is no longer used? Nobody knows how it works? All of this together? Make sure you understand exactly the limitations you will need to face.

Can you get more context on this software?

If this system is being maintained by a team, make sure you talk to them. Understand what their struggles are and try to learn as much as you can from them. If the system is orphaned, try to find people that were involved in the development. Going through some emails and documents and finding some of the business and technical decisions can help untangled some of the unknowns that come with this type of software.

What kind of work it's receiving?

Is this system working with no extra effort? Is someone still fixing some bugs? Has anyone added a big feature recently? Why did they decide to do it? Adding extra features is way harder than fixing bugs, so we need to understand what this system is requiring from the team.

Who is using this system?

This is the most critical question you need to ask. If the legacy system is up and running, it means that it's useful to someone. If it's not, then why is it up anyway? Going to the customers and understanding why they use this system, their likes and dislikes, and how hard it would be for them to move over a new version of it can help you define how much effort you should be investing in trying to build a replacement system.

12.6 Fighting Back on Poor Quality

If you can't just kill the system and start fresh, there's only one way to fight back: refactoring.

Refactoring a codebase is the act of changing it with the intent of making it better without changing any of the original behavior. Sounds good? It is! But don't think it's easy... the problem of making changes on a big codebase—especially a poor quality one—is that you can introduce bugs.

A legacy codebase doesn't have tests, or if it has, they are few and poorly done. The code is very confusing, there's no documentation, and the person who has any idea of anything is long gone. The legacy system is painful, and you can see people rolling their eyes when they need to go back to it. And can you blame them? The lack of tests makes them fragile systems. Any change can be the ultimate crash to ruin everything, and nobody wants to be the doom starter. How can you refactor if there are no tests?

Now we are faced with a dilemma:

"When we change code, we should have tests in place. To put tests in place, we often have to change code."

Refactoring a legacy code is risky, but we need to start somewhere. To minimize problems, we can start by making small changes that are always supported by tests. Ideally, we will write the tests first and make the change after. By writing the tests first, you can guarantee that the refactor didn't change the behavior of the system.

WRITE TESTS ⟶ REFACTOR WHAT'S TESTED ⟶ MAKE SURE TESTS ARE WORKING

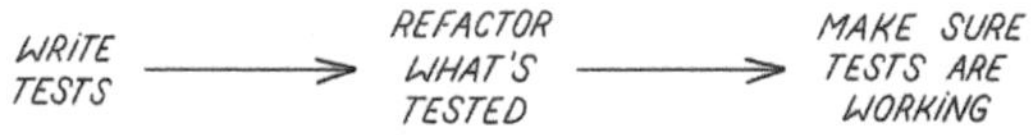

Figure 12-2. *Writing tests before a refactor can guarantee that it didn't change the behavior of the system*

Of course, the preceding scenario is actually a pretty good one: if the code is easy enough to test, the refactoring wasn't *that* hard. In reality, things can get pretty messy. What if there's a huge piece of code that people can barely understand what it does? How can someone ever be able to test it?

One strategy is to find, within the big chunk of untested code, a piece of logic that is (more or less) self-contained—something that could be broken down into a smaller function. You can then extract this piece of code, add tests to it, and use this tested function in the place of the extracted code. Yes, you are still left with a big piece of untested code, but your code is already a bit better than before.

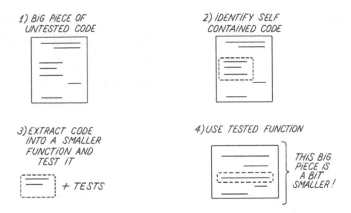

Figure 12-3. *Removing part of a big chunk of untested code into a smaller function that is well tested is a good strategy when the mess is too big to understand and test*

There are several strategies and tons of resources on learning how to deal with, refactor, and improve legacy systems. Legacy systems aren't all a lost cause, but improving them demands resources. Refactoring takes time, is tricky, and doesn't add new features, but it's important work. Everyone should know and value it.

Refactoring doesn't add value to the end user in the short term but is valuable work.

12.7 Learning from Legacy

Although in most of this chapter we discussed how hard it is to deal with legacy systems, there's much we can learn from them, especially when we consider them from a *product* perspective.

More than anything, legacy systems are successful systems. They have been around for a while, and they solve some problems; otherwise, people and businesses wouldn't be using them. It can be an interesting case study to understand what the system was designed for and what it's actually used for.

When building a new product, it's hard to know the customers that might use it. When you have a legacy system, you already have users to talk to. They are relying on this system, and you can gather feedback and precious information about the system and how to improve it. I've heard once that a team fixed a known bug to a legacy system only to find out that the users were using that bug as a feature and the fix decreased the functionality. You can only find out these peculiarities in software that's already in use!

Another thing to consider when you're working with legacy systems is that small improvements can have a large impact, since there are many people using them. Even if you only write tests to a legacy system, you will have an impact because you will decrease the amount of bugs introduced from now on, and less bugs is *always* better.

12.8 What's Next?

Through several iterations, we were able to build the MVP of JollyFarm successfully, and we had a quick look at what could happen if we aren't careful. What's next? As the product is successful, we can iterate on new features, so we need more research, more requirements, and more development cycles! All these need" this to "To do this, you will need resources, so it's time to take a look at one of the most important resources you will need in this journey: the humans.

12.9 Chapter Summary

Developers often face challenges when dealing with existing code. They can be

- **Technical debt**: Areas of code that are prone to bugs or hard to work with because of shortcuts made (typically because of time constraints)

- **Legacy code**: A system that has high business value and low quality and was written by a different person or team

The problem with these challenges is that they decrease the speed in which we can deliver new features and increase the likelihood of bugs. The only way to fight back is to slowly refactor those systems and move them into better states. These quality gains are fairly invisible at first, but they sure pay off in the long run.

12.10 Further Reading

There is a four-minute video where the author of the *Technical Debt* metaphor, Ward Cunningham, explains how he came up with it and some of the context around the creation of the term: `https://fdly.li/12-03`.

I liked the article "10 Challenges To Think About When Upgrading From Legacy Systems" by Forbes Technology Council: `https://fdly.li/12-04`.

Section 9.2 of the book *Software Engineering* by Ian Sommerville (10th edition) has a detailed view on legacy systems and how and when to modify them. Figure 12-1 is actually based on one of the images in this section.

The talk "Prioritizing Technical Debt as if Time and Money Matters" by Adam Tornhill was one of those talks you have to watch multiple times. I absolutely loved it: `https://fdly.li/12-05`.

PART V

Human Aspects of Building Software

CHAPTER 13

A Deeper Look to What Influence Software Teams

Alone a youth runs fast, with an elder slow, but together they go far.

—Luo proverb

For most of this book, we talked about the MVP development of the JollyFarm app. But if we did a good job, there's a chance this story will go on and on to other stages and better and bigger features. Regardless of the moment we talk about—fresh start, scaling, legacy—you will need one or more teams to do the development of this and other products. These teams need to work well together and, hopefully, fix bugs and deliver features with efficiency and quality.

We learned in Chapter 8 that Agile methodologies are the modern way of building software. Is that all we need to worry? The answer, as usual,[1] is no. There is a lot more to build software than just the technical aspects

---

[1] As Betteridge's law of headlines: "Any headline that ends in a question mark can be answered by the word no."

© Leticia Portella 2023
L. Portella, *A Friendly Guide to Software Development*,
https://doi.org/10.1007/978-1-4842-8969-3_13

of it. Efficient and well-adjusted teams have many other factors that will contribute to their success or failure.

Let's assume you have implemented a great Agile methodology; the product requirements are divided into small tasks that are shared among the developers, etc. You expect the product to be delivered well and in time, but the team is struggling and nothing is getting done. What could be wrong?

13.1 On-Call Rotation

As you've seen in Chapter 11, one aspect of having a system running is that it can fail *at any time*. On-call rotation became part of the daily life of modern development. However, this has a major impact on the life of the developer who has to be on-call. A developer who was awake in the middle of the night while debugging and mitigating an issue can't work at 100% speed the next day. If they had no proper rest during the weekends, they will be less productive over the week. If the on-call is a chaotic, constant source of pain, there is no way they can be delivering great work on new features. Your system is drowning and taking the developers with it.

It's important that while you are planning the next features for the JollyFarm, you factor these periods and understand what the developers go through. The team must develop a culture for helping each other if someone needs a shift rotation or a break after a long night. If a pager keeps alerting nonstop, the priority should be to bring the system back to a manageable state. No features should be added until you have something working and a team sleeping well!

13.2 External and Unpredicted Work

Imagine now that there is a big feature that we need to launch by a certain date, so the marketing team can use a conference for getting more users. The team knows what to do, they are focused, and each developer has a deadline to deliver certain parts. Then the team receives a request from another team: there is an urgent update going on, and someone from the team needs to act immediately. Who will do this task?

Nobody will volunteer to handle it because everyone is worried with their own deadlines. No one wants to be the one that didn't deliver a feature because they were busy helping some other team, even when it is on everyone's interest. This doesn't mean that the task is not important! Enough tasks like this, and the team might be in trouble.

Some companies make the on-call developer stop working on feature development and spend the week dedicated to answering and solving these kinds of unpredicted tasks. This means that urgent asks won't go unanswered and important work gets done, even if the whole team has a deadline to achieve. Contrary to on-call pages, these requests are managed during normal working hours, but they can still be quite exhausting as they can be quite demanding. They can also contribute to the overall tiredness that a hard on-call can have on the developers and teams.

13.3 Developer Tools

I once had to do a task that was pretty simple. I looked at the description and confidently said that it would take me half a day. Three days later, I am staring at my computer in frustration, thinking I wanted to cry. Nothing was working. I couldn't even reproduce the steps to get to a point where I could test and see what was happening. My development environment was going crazy, and everything I tried to make it better failed. It took me four days to finally get anything done.

The tools required for a developer to work can have a lot of impact on their productivity (and mental sanity). This can go from things as simple as which program they use to develop code (known as IDE) on their laptops to which kind of programs are used for deploy.

If you have a team that is spending a big chunk of their time struggling with their tools, you are wasting time and money on problems that shouldn't be there. As a developer, it's frustrating when you can't deliver something you said you would, but it's even more frustrating when this happens because your computer keeps freezing or the development environment is behaving unexpectedly. Making sure the developer tools are adequate to the challenges is fundamental.

13.4 Interruptions

Interruptions are part of any work that requires human interaction to solve problems, which is definitely the case of software development. Maybe it's a new person that requires help on a task, maybe it's the weekly team meeting, or maybe it's just something else. It happens, and we need to adjust for this reality. The problem begins when these interruptions get out of hand and people can't control them.

A study[2] showed that people who get interrupted frequently actually perform their task in less time but at a high cost:

> *When people are constantly interrupted, they develop a mode of working faster [...] to compensate for the time they know they will lose by being interrupted. Yet working faster with interruptions has its cost: people in the interrupted conditions experienced a higher workload, more stress, higher frustration, more time pressure, and effort.*

Excess of meetings is a common cause for interruptions, especially when they have a little time between that is not enough time to work on anything relevant. "Defragmenting" calendars is a great strategy to avoid

---

[2] "The cost of interrupted work: more speed and stress" by Gloria Mark, Daniela Gudith, and Ulrich Klocke: https://fdly.li/13-01

these small, unused space of time. Similarly, allowing developers to block their calendar a few times a week or when they have a big project to deliver can help solve part of this problem.

13.5 Interviews

One thing that seems harmless but can take a lot of time is doing interviews. If a single interview can take 1 hour, you still have to consider that the interviewer needs at least 10–15 minutes before the interview to prepare the material, the questions, etc. After an interview, the interviewer has to spend some time writing a consistent feedback. Depending on the company, they have to attend a meeting for deciding among other developers the outcome of that interview process. There you have it: a simple one-hour interview can became an over two-hour appointment.

If you consider that every one-hour interview is actually a two-hour task, over four interviews a week consumed the entirety of an eight-hour workday, transforming the five days a week into a four days a week. And this can be a very conservative estimate. I know people whose teams reserve a half day of work for each interview they are assigned.

You also need to consider that interviews and its subsequent tasks may never occur in sequence; there is the additional cost of context switching that will add stress and frustration to the list of costs. If you are working in a company that is growing very fast and needs tons of interviews, this will need to be included as part of the work, and they can affect deadlines.

13.6 Communication

It's impossible to talk about good and effective teams without addressing the communication aspect of the work. As projects get more complex, multiple teams will be involved in building them. To do that, you will need an enormous amount of communication to make sure all teams are aligned and working toward the same goals. But even in smaller teams, they can only reach the peak of productivity if they communicate well among themselves.

If you look back at Chapter 8, you'll notice that most strategies of Agile methodologies aim to improve and develop communication within the team: the Kanban board allows the team to know what everyone is doing, the pair programming shares knowledge, and Scrum has several ceremonies so people can share context. Even user stories are a tool for communication. What was written in them is less important than the conversation that helped the team understand the user needs.

Sometimes, communication can be as simple as a document. In one of my teams, we created a *decision log*, where every time we had to make a decision that would affect product behavior, we would write it down, and people who agreed on it would "sign off." This way, many months after a decision was made, we could go back in time and understand why things happened the way they did.

Communication is also a big factor why even big companies like to keep teams small. Every new person on the team increases the number of communication lines. For instance, a team with only three developers has three communication lines, while a team of five has nine communication lines!

Figure 13-1. *The more people you have in a single team, the more communication channels will exist, making it harder to get alignment. That's why most companies tend to keep teams small*

One approach to make sure teams are small enough is the Two Pizza Rule[3] in which a team should be small enough that they can be fed with only two pizzas.

Teams that share big areas of code tend to have problems of silos of knowledge, in which only a few people understand certain parts of the codebase. Communication is one of the few ways we can actively fight these silos to happen.

There's a common way of reflecting how much your project has silos of knowledge called the bus factor, which is the number of people that can be hit by a bus before your project is doomed. If this number is one, you are in big trouble.

13.7 Timezones Are Hard

Communication is particularly important when you have timezone differences of more than a couple of hours. Imagine that you have a developer working in Dublin and the rest of the team is in Singapore. In part of the year, there is a nine-hour difference between these places. Some timezones *never* have overlapping working hours.

When building teams and companies across multiple timezones, this can't be overlooked. You can't expect people to have meetings at 11pm constantly. People should be extra careful with everyone's time and lives. There's nothing more frustrating than someone that won't wake up early to help you, making you work late hours if you want to get the job done. Especially if you know that if you don't deliver this, it will be *your* responsibility for missing the deadline.

---

[3] Created by Jeff Bezos while defining teams in Amazon.

Embracing asynchronous communication can help in working on this. However, you can't underestimate how much impact this may have. I once worked in a project with teams in Dublin, Seattle, and Singapore. To respect everyone's timezones, a whole loop of communications would take 24 hours.

13.8 Changing Priorities

One of the most frustrating things of working as a developer is the lack of clear priorities and/or their constant change. If you are working in feature A, then suddenly you need to drop everything because feature B is a priority, but no... actually now it's feature C. Your work is constantly being thrown out the windows, and if everything is important, nothing really is.

Beyond the lack of motivation, chaotic environments like this tend to make developers numb to the urgency of problems. You know you don't really need to hurry and deliver feature C, because by the time you figure out how to do it, something else will have bigger priority.

That said, this doesn't mean that priorities shouldn't change ever. It means that unless it is a real emergency and we need to rethink our goals, we should be careful when hitting the breaks to change directions!

13.9 Glue Work

A well-functioning team is full of other activities that are relevant to the team while still not related to writing code. Things like:

- Writing documentation

- Setting up team meetings

- Establishing code standards

- Improving team processes

- Taking notes during meetings

- Mentoring and coaching

- Onboarding new team members

- Filling user requests

- Organizing off-sites

Tanya Reilly[4] called these glue work: tasks that are indispensable for a team to function well, but can easily go unrecognized.

The major problem with not recognizing glue work is that historically underrepresented groups will volunteer more for it,[5] and while being a usually unrecognized work, it also leads to less promotions. This inevitably leads to minorities being less valued and promoted.

One strategy that worked well in one of my teams was to have a tool that will randomly select one person on the team. Every time we identify a task that was considered glue, we roll the dice and pick a random person on the team. This removes the weight of having to volunteer while distributing the work evenly.

13.10 Team Diversity

When discussing team diversity, people often look at the topic as something that should be done because it's the right thing to do. Indeed, it's the right thing to do—for many, *many* reasons—but it goes beyond it. In fact, many studies reveal that diverse teams make teams more creative and more prepared and even result in higher valuation of companies.[6]

---

[4] https://fdly.li/glue

[5] https://fdly.li/13-02

[6] From the article "How Diversity Makes Us Smarter" by Katherine W. Phillips: https://fdly.li/13-07

Of course, just bringing minority groups into companies and hoping for the best is obviously not going to get you anywhere. It's important to look at bias and make sure everyone is being heard and included. For instance, to make sure everyone in the room gets heard is to make everyone write their ideas before anyone speaks. This way, people that tend to not express their thoughts first can still have a chance to share their points of view, even if they are not the first or the loudest.[7] This is the kind of ideas and thoughtfulness we need if we truly want to work in improving diversity.

13.11 Team Moral and Mental Health

No one should disregard the power of a good team interaction. Google[8] made a research to find what constitutes the perfect team, and the key result was that *who* is on a team matters way less than *how* a team interacts. Good teams are not the ones that have a star developer and a bunch of people that just obey them.

One of the key aspects of a good team dynamic is ensuring that there is psychological safety. When people believe that they will not be punished or humiliated for speaking up with ideas, questions, concerns, or mistakes, people will feel safe in taking risks and showing vulnerability in front of their peers.

13.12 What Now?

We could go on and on here about how to make great teams, but this is definitely not the place, and I am certainly not the person. There are a million things that must be considered when working with a team of

---

[7] Idea from the marvelous book *Thinking, Fast and Slow* by Daniel Kahneman: https://fdly.li/fast-slow
[8] https://fdly.li/13-03

developers, and the topics I wrote here are just a few that I have personally experienced over my career. The "actual" work of developing features and fixing bugs are only a part of the tons of things development teams need to worry, and making sure the development team can adjust and handle the other tasks is as important as anything else.

At this point, we've had several chapters to discuss and understand how software is built, how development teams work, and the challenges they face while trying to juggle it all. However, we haven't actually discussed how the developers see all these and how they expect their role to be in your company. Now it's time we take a deeper look at the people who are at the core of software.

13.13 Chapter Summary

Developers don't spend all of their time writing code, and several things can impact their work and bandwidth to work on new features. Some are easy to see the impact, like constant changing priorities, while others are more subtle. Several interviews a week or multiple sleepless nights due to many pages can be highly impactful. The first can just impact delivery time, while the second can quickly lead to burnout if not properly handled.

One of the key aspects of healthy teams is how teams work together. Things like good communication and psychological safety can have more impact on a team's ability to perform than *who* is on that team. At the end of the day, we are all humans, and we can all work best when we can be ourselves and help each other.

13.14 Further Reading

I highly recommend the blog post (and talk) "Being Glue" from Tanya Reilly (`https://fdly.li/glue`) on how glue work can affect beginners and how minorities usually tend to do this typically unrecognized work.

The book *The Culture Map* by Erin Meyer (https://fdly.li/13-04) is a must read for anyone working in global teams. The author explores how country cultures can create unconscious expectations that can lead to communication failures we don't understand.

The talk "How to Take Great Engineers & Make Them Great Technical Leaders" by Courtney Hemphill is amazing: https://fdly.li/13-05.

I liked the article "5 Things High-Performing Teams Do Differently" by Ron Friedman: https://fdly.li/13-06.

The research from Google on building a successful team was an interesting read to build this chapter: https://fdly.li/13-03.

I highly recommend checking these articles about how diversity improves team dynamics, creativity, and revenue: https://fdly.li/13-07 and https://fdly.li/13-08.

CHAPTER 14

The Role of the Developer

To be a programmer is to develop a carefully managed relationship with error. There's no getting around it. You either make your accommodations with failure, or the work will become intolerable.

—Ellen Ullman

Ah... we finally got to the developers, my crowd. We receive so many names! Software developer, software engineer, programmer, coder. I won't go into the discussion of why there are so many names, but I want to talk about the role of the person that is one of the core pieces on software development.

14.1 What Does a Developer Do Anyway?

Although the first intuition for this question's answer might be simple ("write code"), the truth is that there's much more to be asked from a developer than writing code. When you start your career as a developer, writing code is indeed the most important skill one must have and practice. However, as you start gaining experience, code is part of your

© Leticia Portella 2023
L. Portella, *A Friendly Guide to Software Development*,
https://doi.org/10.1007/978-1-4842-8969-3_14

job, but it can quite easily become a small part. Your projects become bigger, more complex, and less certain. You need to navigate over complex systems and complex people in order to reach the goals you have. Projects can take several months, and meetings can overload the calendar because people will ask for advice and mentoring.

Let's take a look at the expectations of what a developer must do as their career moves forward.

Intern level

People that are studying to become software developers (either via a university course or a <u>bootcamp</u>) can engage in internships to gain practical skills. In some countries, like Brazil, internships are seen as a regular job with less hours. In other countries, like the United States, internships have an end date, and they usually have a single project that will be the intern's responsibility.

At this level, developers are not expected much beyond being able to write small programs in a clear way. Once they join a company, ideally they will have a well-scoped project to work on and a mentor that will be there whenever needed. Interns are expected to ask a lot of questions and to try to learn as much as possible. Because of that, mentors should be expected to have less availability for other projects. However, this experience is also important for mentors as they can use this relationship to start building some skills like scoping a well-defined project, explaining technical concepts in a clear way, and providing clear and consistent feedback.

Figure 14-1. *Internships can be a great way to find amazing developers with huge potential and develop management and technical skills of mentors, which will be more experienced developers*

Although coding will be the main activity of an internship, interns should also be stimulated to learn and develop other relevant skills like the following:

- Learn how to interact and discuss technical challenges

- Learn how to give and receive feedback during code reviews

- Present their project in a clear way to a broader audience

- Learn how to act and escalate problems when they are blocked

- Learn how to communicate effectively with their mentors and peers

It's fundamental to make it clear that interns shouldn't have any practical experience, as this is likely their first. Because of that, companies can use internships to source talent, as if the intern does a good job, they can leave the internship with an offer to come back once they finish their course.

Junior or entry level

This is the level for people that just started working as a full-time software developer or that just have a couple of years of experience. Junior developers should have little to no experience in developing in a real-life environment like a company.

At this level, developers need more "hand holding" and a little uncertainty. Similar to interns, they will need mentors to help clarify their questions and empower them. This is the moment where learning *why* and *how* to do things matter the most. They should be encouraged to learn while they are working, giving them room and confidence to grow.

I still remember the first time I had to do a deploy to production, and I was terrified to do so. My mentor sat near me and showed me that there was nothing scary about it. I was very grateful for how safe he made me feel.

Overall, developers at this level are expected to

- Have good mentors

- Receive well-defined, contained tasks to work on

- Have clear timelines that have room for the developer to work at their own pace

- Receive requirements that are clear, with very little or no unknowns

- Focus on developing their coding skills

- Have time to study and learn

- Be encouraged to ask questions and understand what they are doing

Mid-level

At mid-level, a developer is expected to start working on more complex tasks that have less certainty and more unknowns. They already have a good notion of the codebase and how to navigate through it. At this point, they should start developing problem-solving skills beyond just coding.

This is also the moment where they can start building their path toward becoming a professional that understands the complexity of products and code. The questions they ask start to become more high level, and they can understand the impact of what they do in the overall structure of the system.

They can require help from more experienced colleagues to develop their skills, but they can start leading projects with confidence and independence. They can also help mentor interns and junior developers, using these opportunities to also learn, using the questions to check their knowledge or go after the answer and learn more.

Overall, this role should

- Help less experienced developers with tasks and coding skills

- Deal with more uncertain tasks

- Lead projects that have unknowns

- Improve the complexity and quality of their coding skills

- Learn how to prioritize tasks and deal with timelines

- Start working on their problem-solving skills

Senior level

At a senior level, developers are expected to be problem solvers and handle complex and abstract projects. They can lead bigger projects, and as their experience grows, their projects become less certain, with more variables, maybe multiple teams, and lots of dependencies.

Also, they should work to make sure that all the technical aspects we discussed throughout this book are applied in a way that makes the project sustainable in the long term. They code—sometimes a lot—but they also spend time thinking of technical debt, system architecture, and optimization. They understand the flaws of the system and work with the

251

team to tackle them. They can make reasonable trade-offs between speed of development, technical quality, and time to market of products.

Senior developers are also fundamental to understand how things fall into the big picture of the system. They can understand impact and assess the risks of a decision, always thinking about the future.

Still, they need to dedicate time to make their team better and help grow their teammates. One of the main roles of this job is mentoring and improving the team. A "good" senior that doesn't help less experienced people to thrive will only hurt a team (and there is a whole section dedicated to this later on). Seniors are the role models of the team, and they need to be up to the task.

Figure 14-2. *Senior developers can deal with a lot of unknowns, leading complex projects with lots of moving parts. They are also role models for the rest of the team, mentoring less experienced developers and pushing the team to build high-quality systems*

A senior developer is expected to

- Be problem solvers

- Lead big projects with lots of unknowns and moving pieces

- Deliver good and clear code, always aiming for improving quality

- Push the team to have a sustainable codebase

- Understand how things are related in the overall system they develop on

- Give great feedback, either on the code, on the architecture and design of the system, or on the career

- Be a great mentor to others

A senior developer is typically a career stage, meaning that people are not expected to go beyond this level. Junior and mid-level developers have an expectation for improvement, and there is a risk of not moving forward on those levels, but senior developers don't have the same pressure. They could continue climbing up the ladder, but it's up to them what they prefer to do.

Principal level

A principal developer, also known as a *staff developer*, is when the developer is expected to be *extremely* experienced, and their focus shifts a bit. At this level, they should have enough experience to lead the most complicated projects and help lead the company. This means that they will be doing things like developing strategies to deal with company-wide projects and guidelines. They need to be able to navigate uncertainty, to help guide multiple teams toward the right path, and deal with highly abstract projects.

If senior developers are expected to be mentors to others, this is even more true to principal developers. They are the leaders and the ones that will help others get more experience and do their jobs even better. As a balance, they are not expected to produce as much code as a senior developer. They can invest their time in producing proof of concepts and prototypes that might never see the light of day.

At this level, the developer is expected to be highly experienced, but they can be experienced on different things. Some companies use archetypes to allow principal developers to grow within the level by working with their

253

strengths and on projects they like. All archetypes have their value, so they shouldn't be compared but instead used to realize the place for each one of them within the company. In general, there are two main divisions:

- **The specialist**: The ones who deeply understand a part of the system that is critical, but they might not have a lot of experience in the whole codebase. They are bounded to a specific area, but completely mastered it. They are fundamental people to develop deep expertise and build reliable systems.

- **The generalist**: These are the developers that have broad knowledge about the system, products, and use cases. They understand how different parts of the system work together and their areas of friction. They are fundamental on leading cross-functional projects, where different teams have to work together.

Figure 14-3. *At the principal level, developers can be experienced on different things, either going deeply into a single topic or knowing a bit of everything. These archetypes are not to be compared, but be leveraged to use the best skills in the right problems*

Where are the principals?

A lot of companies don't give options for developers to continue to grow technically after the senior level. In these companies, the only possible choice for moving up is to switch to a manager position. As you can imagine, this is not something that every developer wants. Principal levels allow developers to continue to grow in their career even if they decide they want to continue to be developers and not managers. Even if you consider companies where the manager is highly technical, the skills and problems required for that job might not be what certain developers want. I remember I saw a great quote[1] that goes like this:

> *Take a great developer and promote them to a manager and you might lose a great developer and gain a bad manager.*

When a company offers an option to follow a career either becoming more specialized (principal level) or becoming a manager, we say it has a Y career, where each person can choose the path that is best for them.

14.2 Which Level Am I?

Levels are a complicated thing. While a developer in a small company can be considered a senior, in another company they might enter as a mid-level role. I view levels as something that is more relevant to a company expectation than to define someone's career. If a person is moving from a small company, with very few developers and not-so-complex projects, to a big company with lots of complex projects, their level can be impacted, but that doesn't mean they are taking a step back!

---

[1] Couldn't find the original source.

I have talked to many "junior" developers that were leading projects because they were the only person available at a company. At one point in time I considered myself at a certain level but accepted a lower level position because I really thought the opportunity was worth it.

One common mistake is to dictate levels based on years of experience. As a famous phrase would say[2]

> *10 years of experience could simply mean a 1-year experience repeated 10 times.*

There's a level of pride on levels and titles, for sure, but they shouldn't measure the level of impact and importance of a developer. At the end of the day, developers want challenging projects that they can learn and improve their skills and fair recognition that they are doing a good job. Levels can be a way to get the latter, but not the only one.

14.3 The Fallacy of the Superhero Developer

It's time to discuss the most annoying and discouraging figure that exists in the popular imagination of the tech world: the image of the lonely, can-solve-anything, transform-coffee-into-code superhero developer. Yes, they only exist in the popular imagination.

The problem with trying to find the one developer to conquer them all is that this thinking is, in essence, naive. Believing that you will find one person that will be the single solution to every problem ignores so many aspects of software development. As we discussed throughout this book, there is far too much for a single person to be able to do it all by themselves.

---

[2] I searched for the original quote but didn't find the original author: https://fdly.li/14-01

Let's imagine the following scenario: there is a major problem in a codebase that has no tests to it. The superhero is called to rescue and fix the problem in a bat of an eye, and 100 lines of code are pushed directly into production. Now comes the question: Are they a hero?

We can quickly notice that

- The code was added without tests, so we can't guarantee it works properly.

- The code was not peer reviewed, so we can't attest for the code quality.

- The codebase continues to be the domain knowledge of that single developer.

This is clearly not a hero, but a liability. I particularly like this quote on Quora that answered the question "What is a hero programmer?":[3]

> *Someone who would rather jump and fix a problem under pressure than doing the structural work to prevent the problem from happening in the first place.*

> —Pal Hargitai

There is also a false idea that a team of superhero developers will become a superstar team, and that's not true. To be highly productive, a team shouldn't focus on individuals, but on a team. As we've seen in Chapter 13, things like psychological safety and structure are more relevant than superstars. If your superhero is making people uncomfortable and afraid to ask questions, they are actually diminishing the overall productivity while becoming the so feared bottleneck.

---

[3] I like this quote although I disagree with the rest of the answer that says that a true hero exists: https://fdly.li/14-02

The "ideal" developer is not the one who will magically solve everything by themselves in a corner of some dark room. They are there to help fix things when times are critical, but in the meantime they are assuring the quality and processes that make software and everyone's life better. They are a team player first of all:[4]

> *Software development is more like rowing. It's a team sport that requires skill and synchronization. This applies at all scales. On a three-person boat, one person out of sync will stall your boat. As you get bigger, no single developer can impact your team's performance, so synchronization is key. Making your team as efficient as possible is what determines long-term success.*
>
> —Avichal Garg

Make sure the team is working well together and that a single superhero isn't making a great team worse.

Figure 14-4. Good senior developers understand they are part of a team and that the team's success is their success

---

[4] https://fdly.li/14-03

14.4 The "Soft" Skills

There's a common way of talking about the professional skills of a software developer that divide between technical and nontechnical skills. The technical skills, like coding, software architecture, etc., are called hard skills, while other traits, like good communication, critical thinking, public speaking, etc., are called soft skills.

For a long time, the technical skills were considered the most important skill a developer should have. That's the main origin of the superhero developer myth, as being able to solve any technical problem was perceived like the only "real" skill. As we discussed in the previous section, software development is a *team* effort, and working with humans requires a different set of skills.

I particularly like the following phrase:[5]

> *As a developer you are problem solver, code might just be how you do that.*
>
> —Matt Brunt

Real-life problems require multiple people to work together to solve them, and these are not machines working together. They are humans! Coding is just a tool to solve problems, not the ultimate goal. This means that the soft skills are becoming more relevant by the day.

There's an intrinsic problem with the word "soft" skills,[6] which can easily be confused with "easy" or "dispensable." The reality is that learning how to work with computers is much more straightforward than working with humans, and there's nothing easy on these skills. Of course, some people are better at them while others struggle, but we need everyone to

---

[5] "Dungeons, Dragons & Developers" by Matt Brunt: `https://fdly.li/14-04`
[6] I've heard some people calling it meta-skills.

259

actively appreciate and develop these skills. If we are not able to work with other humans, how can we create amazing and complex projects?

14.5 Where Are the Juniors?

OK, so now it's time to address a topic I dislike even more than the superhero developer myth: the "I only hire seniors." It's not hard to find companies that use this posture and think it is the most clever thing ever. This is completely and utterly nonsense, and I want to talk about it.

First of all, they are losing money. Not all tasks that have to be done require the best, top-level developer in the room. You will have that not-so-complicated task that can be solved by a more junior developer (that typically costs less) while you dedicate your best and most expensive resources to the most complex tasks.

Secondly, they are losing a big pool of amazing developers that can be more easily sourced than developers that have been around for a while. Some junior developers are great, and they just need a chance to prove themselves. Isn't it better to give them the first opportunity and have them around because they have a great environment to grow?

Also, this shows how much this company's culture is rotten. Early career developers can make more mistakes, which means that you have to have better processes, good mentoring, and guidance to prevent these mistakes. But you also need to embrace that mistakes are part of life. Living in a company that doesn't allow mistakes is very intimidating and can highly affect mental health. As we've seen in Chapter 11, gigantic mistakes are never a single person's fault. Anything different from that means a bad, bad culture.

Finally, junior developers also have an extremely important job in a team:[7]

---

[7] *Managing a Data Science Team* at https://fdly.li/14-05

Don't just hire senior people. Not only are they in high demand and expensive, but less experienced employees have the "luxury of ignorance" and can ask "dumb" questions. These questions are not actually dumb, of course, but are unencumbered by the usual assumptions that more experienced professionals stop being aware they are making. It's not hard to become infatuated with a particular way of doing things and to forget to question whether a favored approach is still the best solution to a new task.

—Angela Bassa

Create internships, hire junior developers, and make sure you have good seniors to mentor them into being their best. You can only gain from such interactions.

14.6 The Ideal Team

In most of this chapter, I discussed levels of developers more or less as if this is the only aspect that matters when hiring developers. The reality is that there are many more nuances than just this. You can have a senior developer who is a really good debugger and can find the problems just by a quick look; others will be really, really good at asking questions and raising problems way before they are even close; and others will just push for better documents and processes. The different skills and traits can vary wildly, even if you consider only senior developers.

If correctly channeled, having these diverse skills can only be beneficial as teams can leverage them and cover all possible areas at the same time.

I once was invited to join a team that was very early in the process of starting a project. I was considered an entry-level developer in the company, and that was an amazing opportunity but a hard one. Everyone had many more years of experience than me! What would I even do there?

I spent a long time talking to people and trying to understand the reasons why they chose me. What I discover was that they valued some other characteristics I have—like empathy and good communication—and that this would be important while building a team from scratch, even if I was not as experienced as the other developers.

The summary is pretty simple: hire a diverse team. Hire different levels of developers, with different skills and different traits. Hire people from different backgrounds (and race, gender, etc.). You can only make things better, not only for the team but for the system as well.

14.7 Chapter Summary

Developers are intrinsically problem solvers, and code is just a tool they use to solve problems. Just as important as technical skills, things like communication, empathy, teamwork (often called "soft" skills) are fundamental to solve big problems, and they become more important by the day.

One of the most dreadful things is the definition of levels. What makes a "senior" developer? Levels have more to do with company expectations of a developer rather than the developer themselves. A senior developer in a company can be a mid-level in another that has bigger and more complex projects. What matters is that developers see a path of growth, even if they, in theory, need to take a step back on the title.

While building a team of developers, diversity is key: a diverse set of levels, skills, traits, backgrounds, etc. Teams can use individual strengths to complement each other, pushing the team and the system to be way better than they would otherwise!

14.8 Further Reading

The talk "Dungeons, Dragons & Developers" by Matt Brunt is a great overview of how you need a team of developers with different personalities, and strength is the best way of getting to a great team: https://fdly.li/14-04.

Although the post "Focus on building 10x teams, not on hiring 10x developers" by Avichal Garg is over ten years old, I found an excellent read, which is still very relevant: https://fdly.li/14-03.

If you are someone in the beginning of a career in programming or if you are mentoring one, the "So you want to be a wizard" guide from Julia Evans is a great way to learn about things all developers need to deal with: https://fdly.li/14-06.

Will Larson created a whole website (and a book!) dedicated to Staff Developers stories and what is expected of such role: https://fdly.li/14-07.

I found the post "If you don't hire juniors, you don't deserve seniors" by Isaac Lyman to be an excellent discussion about the pitfalls of a seniors-only culture: https://fdly.li/14-08.

CHAPTER 15

Building Software Is More Than Developers

While writing code can be a solitary act, making software isn't.

—Duretti Hirpa

With a few exceptions, this book discusses work that is typically executed by developers. This is on purpose, as I focused on demystifying the *technical side* of a software product. However, there is a common assumption that the software industry is basically composed of developers.

Although developers are at the core of the software industry, as they are the ones who write code, software can't be built by developers alone. Good software require a myriad of people with different skills, and developers are just one of the roles we need, but definitely not the only one.

When we started the JollyFarm, a couple of developers and a single manager were more than enough to get the MVP out of the paper. We might have used a developer that has strong design skills or another that could also help with creating an amazing product. This is very useful at early stages, both because it's financially more adequate to rocky starts and it can also allow us to move fast, as when you have less people you need to communicate with.

© Leticia Portella 2023
L. Portella, *A Friendly Guide to Software Development*,
https://doi.org/10.1007/978-1-4842-8969-3_15

However, even if you get the best Swiss Army Knife person in the world, they can never be as good as a team of specialized professionals. It's like asking for a general practitioner to operate on a heart. They might have an idea on how to do the surgery, but you can't expect it to go as well as with a specialist, right?

As our software is a success, it will evolve and grow so we need to start calling the experts. In this chapter, we will discuss some of the experts we can rely on to make our product even better.

15.1 The Role of the Managers

In this section, we will discuss the role of managers and how they can influence software projects and teams. Although we divide this section into different roles, most companies don't have the resources or don't need such divisions, and a single manager can do a bit of everything.

15.1.1 The Developer Manager

As with anyone, each developer has their own strengths, areas to grow, things they like, and things they hate. They need a person that will help match the project's and companies' plans with the plans they have for their own careers. The developer manager is the person that can help the team of developers to meet their deadlines while still caring about their careers and their wishes.

The developer manager makes sure the developer team is operating at its best capacity, having impact, and that each developer is progressing in their careers.

For instance, one time my manager assigned me to a task that I thought wouldn't match with the things I wanted to improve in my career. During our weekly meeting, I told him about this, and we discussed some possibilities. In the following week, he agreed to move me to a different project that was more aligned with what I wanted and made sure that I had enough support on that project so I could learn but still meet the deadlines. This required moving people around projects, and I can only think this probably looks like playing chess when all pieces have feelings about where they are in the board.

There's no agreement if developer managers should be developers that migrated to a management position or not. As they deal with a lot of career development, some defend that they could be from a "less technical" background and still be excellent managers, while others disagree on that. Some companies can add a role of a tech lead as someone that takes care of the system while the developer manager takes care of the team and the people in it.

This quote by Charity Major explains a bit about the difference between a tech lead and a developer manager:[1]

> *Management is highly interruptive, and great engineering— where you're learning things—requires blocking out interruptions. [...] As a manager, it's your job to be available for your team, to be interrupted. It is your job to choose to hand off the challenging assignments, so that your engineers can get better at engineering.*
>
> —Charity Major

---

[1] "The Engineer/Manager Pendulum" by Charity Major: https://fdly.li/15-01

In general, developer managers should know the answers to these questions for each developer on their team:

- What are they working on?

- In which area do they like/dislike to work on?

- Are they feeling satisfied with the current work?

- Are they learning what they want to?

- What are they trying to improve in themselves?

- Who can lead the ambitious project that the team will have in a couple of months?

15.1.2 The Product Manager

The product manager (known as PM) is responsible for the long-term vision of a product and its customers. This role aims to make sure that the product has the right product-market fit and can grow successfully over time. They need to know the answers to questions like the following:

- Are we building the right features?

- Are our customers happy with our product?

- Which feature should we build next to optimize user adoption?

- What can we do to get more users to adopt our product?

Product managers also help the team align on priorities, keeping the focus and making sure that the developers are working on relevant features, correctly prioritized. In fact, some of what we discussed in Chapter 2 is related to the expertise of product managers, like defining the target user and the requirements for an MVP.

Product managers make sure that the teams are working on the
things that will solve the customer's needs.

It's important to state how much *influence* a product manager can and
should have on their team:[2]

> As product managers, it's easy to get stuck in making all the
> decisions. The questions keep coming in and it can feel great to
> help move your team forward by making the decisions, but
> they quickly pile up and leave you with no time to consider the
> bigger picture.
>
> If there is one thing that I've seen that works consistently, it's
> this: Shared understanding massively multiplies decision-
> making velocity. Instead of making the decision yourself, take
> the time to develop your whole team's understanding of the
> customer, the vision, and the strategy of your product.
>
> —Sherif Mansour

The product manager can influence the team's mindset and then let
the team make better day-to-day decisions, while they can focus on the big
picture and the future of the product.

15.1.3 The Project Manager

As a product manager aims to define "what will we build" on a product,
that doesn't mean that they will be involved in a single *project*. Several
projects can be happening to develop a single product, and as any other
project, we still need someone to see the execution of these projects. This
is the role of a project manager (confusingly also known as a PM).

---

[2] "Product managers make all the decisions... right?" by Sherif Mansour in
`https://fdly.li/15-02`

The project manager is the person who can help teams deliver projects on time and within budget. They are responsible to handle stakeholders' interests, cross-functional team work, deadlines, budget, etc. They also define (or help to define) the success criteria of the projects, making sure everyone aims to work on the right things to be able to finish the project.

In tech companies, the project manager tends to be closer to the development team, being highly technical themselves, and they are sometimes called a Technical Program Manager (TPM).

The TPM will help drive projects from scoping to delivery, define milestones, and align the team's expectations. They can lead complex projects that have tons of moving parts, being able to quickly act to mitigate risks and escalate problems, when necessary. They need to know the answers to questions like the following:

- Which team is responsible for which part of this project?

- Is the project on track?

- Which deliverables are behind? Will this affect the overall deadline of this project?

- Is any team blocked?

- Which risks we need to mitigate?

Technical Program Managers (TPM) help the organization to deliver critical projects successfully.

I really liked this image to explain the difference between the roles of the product manager, TPM, and developer manager:[3]

---

[3] Based on an image in the article "What TPMs Do and What Software Engineers Can Learn From Them" by Gergely Orosz: https://fdly.li/15-03

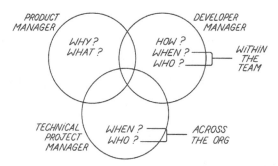

Figure 15-1. *The difference between the product manager, Technical Program Manager (TPM), and developer manager. Based on:* https://fdly.li/15-03

15.2 The Role of the Business Specialist

The product manager will typically have a lot of insights on the business area that the software product is aiming to help. However, some businesses can benefit (or even require) a person that is specialized in that area.

For instance, as good as product managers may be, if they are building a software for the legal area or taxes, these topics are way too dense for an "outsider" to drive some particulars.

That's when we call the business specialist (also known as a subject matter expert). These are people who spent their careers in a specific field (like lawyers), and they know *a lot* about their fields. They will guide the business aspects of the product, making sure edge cases are well thought out, the caveats are avoided, and the product is doing the right job.

Business specialists help drive niche products where the subject matter is way too dense for unspecialized people to fully understand.

Because they (usually) don't have a product background, the product manager will be the bridge between what they say and what the development team will act on. They need to make sure the business suggestions make sense from a product perspective, how they will impact the customers and how much priority they have.

15.3 The Role of the Designer

The designer is responsible for improving the human-computer interaction. They study, plan, and design how people and programs work together so that the user's needs are satisfied in the most effective way. They must consider things like the following:

- What does a person want from the experience?
- What physical limitations and abilities people possess?
- How do they interact with a product?
- What do people find enjoyable?
- What are the main problems they face?

Some of the things we discussed in Chapter 2 are also related to the expertise of designers, like the user research and the definition of the personas.

The role of the designer can be further subdivided into two areas: the user interface (UI) and the user experience (UX).

The UI designer focuses on the aesthetics of a product. The color palettes, the font type, and how things are displayed in the product are just some of the things this role is worried about.

The user interface designer creates products that delight users aesthetically.

The UX designer focuses on how a user moves from point A (where they are) to point B (where they wish to be) most effectively. This can be both on software products and on IOT devices as well. Part of their work is going to the users, understanding how they interact with a product, learning their problems, and making sure that the product is building the things they need, rather than what someone else think they need.

The user experience designer creates products that delight users because of their effectiveness.

15.4 The Role of the Data Analyst

In today's world, if you are still making decisions based on intuition, the business is probably falling behind. Data is gold, and the only way to get to it is by analyzing and crunching numbers. The data analyst can help understand the metrics and drive decisions through their discoveries. They help get the data to answer questions like the following:

- Which kind of customers are using our product?

- What is driving the growth/decrease of our product usage?

- How many of our customers are cancelling the product?

- What is the monthly/annual recurring revenue?

- In which part of the funnel customers are getting stuck?

Data analysts look for answers in the data to drive the product and business decisions.

They also need to understand *if* they have the data to answer the questions they have and how to get the data, if it doesn't exist already. Once the team starts getting answers, there is a high chance that more questions will arrive, and the data analyst will need to get deeper and deeper into the data. In fact, they can open the door to a whole area of data science that could be a whole book by itself!

15.5 The Role of the Customer Support

As your software starts to have customers and users, they will have doubts, find bugs, and ultimately need help one time or another. Even if your team is trying to do their best to create the best product ever, this is only natural. You need someone to help deal with this load. They need to be empathetic enough to acknowledge the frustrations and technical enough that they can help with the most common problems. This is the role of customer support, and they have invaluable importance in helping your customers to feel heard and supported.

They also provide a shield to the team that is working on the development of the product. As the product grows and more and more people start using it, the amount of requests from users can (and probably will) increase exponentially and quickly overload the development team to a point that they can't really work on improving the product, just answer tickets.

Customer support makes sure that customers are well supported when they need help.

15.6 The Role of the Technical Writer

As we've learned in Chapter 9, documentation is an important part of software projects, but writing it is not an easy task. It not only requires technical expertise but also knowledge of writing techniques. As with anything, developers might be expected to write some documentation, but it's not their main focus or main skill. The professional that can properly work with documentation is the technical writer.

This professional will address questions such as the following:

- Who is the audience of the documentation?

- How do they typically interact with the product?

- Why do they need this software?

- What is the audience's knowledge level?

Once they understand these topics, they will be responsible for writing the appropriate documentation, organize it in a way that it will be discovered in the order that it will be used, and so on. Similarly to the designer, the technical writer will go to users and find their pain points while using the documentation and iterate with them to create better docs.

Technical writers make sure the information is transmitted clearly and effectively to the intended audience.

Although typically used to create amazing docs to external users, technical writers can be very useful for internal communications as well. As companies grow, sharing information within the company can be as big of a task as writing for an external audience.

15.7 The Role of... You!

Congratulations! You've been through a whole product cycle and now have a successful product with tons of people using it! Yay!

As you learned in this book, developers might be the most known actor in the software industry, but they are only one element of a big industry. Technology can only be effective in solving real-life problems if we have different perspectives and talents. Expecting a single type of profession and/or personality to be the one solution to all our problems is a naive and utterly ineffective approach.

Bringing different perspectives to the table can only improve the results and will broaden the audience that those solutions reach. Technology can't solve people's problems without *people* being involved in the conversation and development, and that means you! Our world is far too beautiful and complex to be "solved" by a single group of people. Shall we join the conversation?

15.8 Further Reading

The Phoenix Project by Gene Kim, Kevin Behr, and George Spafford is a great (and fun) read about the struggles of a manager that is pulled into a late project where everything is on fire. The main character needs to work with several people with different skills to try getting things back on track: `https://fdly.li/phoenix`.

The classic post "How to Hire a Product Manager" by Ken Norton is brilliant (`https://fdly.li/15-04`), but I would also highly recommend the article "Liberal Arts and Technical Enoughness," where they discuss the need for PMs to be technical enough: `https://fdly.li/15-05`.

The blog post "What TPMs Do and What Software Engineers Can Learn From Them" by Gergely Orosz is a great source to understand the difference between critical roles that are close to developers: `https://fdly.li/15-03`.

The book *The Manager's Path* by Camille Fournier is a great read for anyone that wants to climb the management path in tech companies. Each chapter discusses a specific role (manager, manager of managers, etc.), so you can choose to read only the chapter that applies to what you want to do: `https://fdly.li/15-06`.

The zine "Help! I have a manager!" by Julia Evans is a great read for people that need to learn better communication with their managers: `https://fdly.li/15-07`.

I also found this comparison between a tech lead and an engineering manager to be quite interesting: `https://fdly.li/15-08`.

Glossary

Agile Manifesto A set of values that proposed how code should be done in order to have more successful projects and deliver products that mattered. It was created in 2001 by a group of 13 developers.

Agile philosophy A set of principles for developing software products that focus on short iterations and constant customer feedback.

algorithm A set of instructions that should be executed in an order, similar to a cooking recipe.

Android An open source mobile operating system mainly sponsored by Google.

application software A software that is specialized on some task such as rendering a photo or editing a text.

atomic transaction A series of steps in a transaction where either they all happen successfully or none of them does. A good example is a money transaction: money can't leave a bank account but never arrive in another.

authentication A process to guarantee that who is making a request is who they say they are.

backend The backend is every logic and system that the final user doesn't directly interact with but is highly dependent on.

backlog A list of tasks, features, bugs, and improvements that should or could be added to a system.

backup A copy from an original data that is stored in a different place in order to guarantee that all the data isn't lost if something happens to the original database.

© Leticia Portella 2023
L. Portella, *A Friendly Guide to Software Development*,
https://doi.org/10.1007/978-1-4842-8969-3

big data A type of software infrastructure to deal with an enormous amount of data. Typically used when data can't fit or be processed by a single computer.

bootcamp An intensive course where a person can learn how to become a software developer. It can take from weeks to months and is focused on the practical experience of a developer rather than the theory behind computer science (as universities do).

browser A software application that allows the user to access the Internet.

bug A defect in a code or algorithm.

bus factor The number of developers that must be hit.

business logic All the information a user gains by using a system.

canary release See incremental rollout.

client Any device that allows a user to connect to the Internet such as a tablet, a browser, a cellphone, a TV, etc.

cloud infrastructure When a system uses remote computers over the Internet rather than a local computer. Cloud services are usually provided by hosting providers.

code The result of writing a programming language to perform an algorithm.

code review A process where whenever someone wants to add a new code to the codebase, the code will be reviewed by someone else in the team.

codebase The files and folders that make up a software.

commit A "package" containing a code change that was introduced to the codebase. It contains the code change as well as who wrote it and when.

Continuous Delivery Developing code in small incremental changes instead of one big change at a time.

Continuous Deployment As soon as the code reaches the main repository, it can be automatically and safely deployed in production.

CRUD A series of the basic operations one must consider while dealing with data: create, retrieve, update, and delete.

data center A building or a room in a building that is dedicated to store computers in safe conditions such as room temperature, humidity, Internet connection, etc.

data locality When there is a restriction that some data must be used and stored in the same place. Typically imposed by countries to protect the consumer's privacy.

database Systems that are designed for storing and finding information (data).

database schema How tables and information are organized in a relational database.

debug The process of finding the root cause of a bug.

deploy The process of moving a software from the development stage to the production stage.

devbox Same as development environment.

development environment The environment where a code program is being created; thus, it is still not available to users. Also known as the development stage or devbox.

domain The "name" part of a URL such as "wikipedia" in *wikipedia. org*. It's also used to refer to the combination of domain and top-level domain such as *wikipedia.org*.

dynamic website A website where the information depends on and changes with the user that is using the system.

dynamically typed language A programming language that doesn't require the developer to write which type each variable is (such as an integer or a float number) before ever running the code.

e2e A type of test that aims to represent exactly what the user goes through, making sure that all parts work as the user expects.

endpoint A part of the server that can handle a specific request.

feature A new functionality that is added to a software.

feature flag A strategy where a new feature is kept behind a gate. You can onboard users to this new feature slowly, as you gain more confidence that everything is working correctly.

float number A number that contains decimal digits such as 6.25. An alternative to integer numbers.

framework A language-specific tool that comes with features prebuilt and ready for a developer to build on top of while guaranteeing some features that are needed regardless of the reasons why a system was built.

framework extensibility How easy it is to create additional tools and adapt an existing framework.

frontend Area of the system that is responsible for managing user interaction.

function Some piece of code that receives inputs, works with them internally, and returns one or more outputs.

git The main tool used for software versioning where you can see what was built, when, and by whom.

GitHub A platform for code sharing and development that uses Git, similar to GitLab.

GitLab A platform for code sharing and development that uses Git, similar to GitHub.

glue work Tasks that are indispensable for a team to function, but can easily go unrecognized like writing documentation, writing notes, and mentoring.

hard skills Technical skills, like coding and software architecture. Complemented by soft skills.

hardware The physical part of a technological device.

hosting provider A company that rents a computer so you can run your software on it.

HTML A markup language that can be applied to pieces of text to give them different meaning.

HTML tag A set of symbols that indicate how the items that are between the two tags should be interpreted.

HTTP body The area in an HTTP message that contains information that a server should process. Usually filled with user information.

HTTP headers The area in an HTTP message that contains metadata about the message being sent on the body.

HTTP message See HTTP request and HTTP response.

HTTP method A verb, usually indicated as an upper case, that specifies which kind of action is expected from a server.

HTTP request A message sent in a specific format that must have at least an HTTP method and a path, but can contain a body and headers.

HTTP response A message sent back from a server after it received an HTTP request. It usually contains a three-digit status code.

IDE Acronym for Integrated Development Environment, the tool developers use to write code. It typically has additional tools that help increase productivity.

incident An event caused by a fault or a failure where something didn't perform the way it should.

incident severity A scale in which a developer can classify the impact of an incident.

incremental rollout A deployment strategy where you start directing a small percentage of users to the new system version and keep increasing the percentage as you get more confident that the system is healthy.

integer number A number that doesn't contain decimals such as 1 or 2. An alternative to float numbers.

integration test A type of test where we check if multiple parts are working together. They are more complex than unit tests and less broad than e2e tests.

iOS A proprietary mobile operating system developed by Apple.

IP address A unique identification of a computer on the Internet. It's a sequence of four numbers, each varying from 0 to 255, separated by dots, such as 192.45.3.29.

iteration Synonym of a cycle of something that gets repeated.

Java A popular backend programming language. Don't confuse it with JavaScript.

JavaScript A mainly frontend programming language that allows you to implement complex features on web pages. Don't confuse it with Java!

Kanban board A board where developers can visualize their work. It can have multiple columns including a backlog column, a Work in Progress column, and a Done column.

landing page A web page where users can learn about a product, even if the product is still under development.

latency How long it takes for a request to reach a server and be back. Usually measured in milliseconds.

latency test A test where you simulate high loads in the system to see how long it takes to respond.

legacy system An old system (and code) that usually doesn't follow clean code guidelines nor have an extensive test suite, making it extremely hard to maintain.

libraries Packages that are written in a programming language that can be used to make a part of programming easier.

load test A test where you simulate a high number of requests in a software in order to test its limits under a high load.

log A text that is stored to help understand how a system was working at a particular time. It can indicate an action that was taken, a situation that occurred, etc.

maintainability Writing software in a way that it can easily be changed and evolve with time.

metadata Metadata refers to a kind of data that gives information about other data.

microservices architecture When features of a product are distributed in several smaller systems that work together. The opposite of monolith architecture.

modularity How a system is divided into well-distributed pieces with clear boundaries, making it easy to maintain and test.

monolith architecture When all features of a product is in a single system. The opposite of microservices architecture.

Multipage Application Every different web page of a website must be sent from a server to a client when requested. Opposite of SPAs.

MVP A small project, with few but important features that will be used to validate a product.

native application A mobile application that is written in the priority programming language of a mobile operating system.

natural A human language, such as English, Spanish, Portuguese, etc.

non-native application A mobile application that is written in one language but can be used no matter which mobile operating system the user is using.

NoSQL databases Highly performing databases with unstructured data. They can be of various different types like document and graph databases.

on-call When a developer is alert to respond to a problem that occurred in the system. They must be with their computers and access to internet at all times.

operating system A type of software that is specialized in interacting with hardware and that allows application programs to run on top of it.

p95 Related to latency. In 100 requests, 95 will be under the p95 value.

p99 Related to latency. In 100 requests, 99 will be under the p99 value.

pair programming When two developers work together on a single problem.

persona A realistic character sketch representing one segment of a targeted audience.

pivot When a company decides to change their business model.

postmortem A document that details the who, what, where, when, and why of incidents after they occur.

production environment The environment where a system is available to users. Also known as the production stage.

program When a code can be executed by a computer, it becomes available as a program.

programming language A language that allows people to communicate instructions to computers.

queries When you go to a database and extract relevant data to analyze.

recommendation system A system uses the previous behavior of similar users to recommend things they would like to buy or watch.

refactoring The act of changing it with the intent of making it better.

relational database A database where information is stored in structured schemas and divided into tables. Data can be queries with SQL. Also known as SQL databases.

relationship When referring to a database, it regards the connection between two tables of a database. A Book table can have a relationship with an Author table, because you can attach an Author to a Book and several Books with an Author.

relative URL When a URL is represented using only the paths rather than the full URL.

release version When several changes made to a codebase are deployed together, in one massive deploy. Opposite to Continuous Deployment.

reliability When a system works correctly even in the face of adversity (hardware or software faults, human errors, etc.).

requirement The list of things that a software must have. They can vary from highly abstract (user requirements) to highly technical (system requirements).

responsive website A website that can be adapted to the size of the screen it's being displayed on, regardless if it is a small phone or a huge monitor.

rollout Same as the deploy.

root Used to describe the main area of something. When referred to websites, it's used to represent the initial page a user will see.

scalability The property of a system to handle a growing amount of requests without failing or lowering performance.

script An algorithm that lives in a single file.

Scrum An Agile methodology that breaks the deployment cycle into sprints of a couple of weeks (typically 2).

search engine A web software dedicated to finding information on other websites.

server A software application that is prepared to receive requests from clients and respond to them.

Single-Page Application A website with a complex frontend, when the first request gets all the tools to build the website and the following requests can be just data.

soft skills Nontechnical yet fundamental skills for developers like good communication, public speaking, emotional intelligence, etc.

software The virtual, abstract part of a technological device. In practical terms, it consists of a program and other tangible (documentation) and intangible (rules and procedures) parts.

software architecture The way a system is designed, including the relationship between a server and a client, fault tolerance, etc.

sprint A development cycle that can be from a single week to a month.

SQL A language to query data from relational databases.

SQL database Same as the relational database.

SQL injection A type of attack where an ill-intended user adds SQL commands to form inputs in order to harm a system, such as deleting a table.

standup A typical daily and quick meeting where everyone in the team gets enough idea to know what is happening and what are the problems their colleagues are facing.

static website A website that will always display the same content regardless of the user and moment in time.

statically typed language A programming language that requires the developer to write which type each variable is (such as an integer or a float number) before ever running the code.

status code A three-digit number that indicates the status in response to an HTTP request message.

string A sequence of characters interpreted as a text. See more in variable.

subdomain An optional part of the URL that comes before the domain. For instance, *en* in the URL en.wikipedia.org.

technical debt Code that is more complicated than it should be and can easily create delays because it's harder to understand and/or prone to bugs.

test suite The different layers of test (unit test, integration, end to end) that help add reliability to a system.

to run When a program or script is executed by the computer.

top-level domain A part of the domain as *.com*, *.org*, or *.eu*. There are over 1500 top-level domains as of 2021.

Two Pizza Rule A team should be small enough that two pizzas can feed the entire team.

unit test A test that isolates each part of a program and verifies it works correctly.

uptime The percent of a year that a system is expected to be working.

URL A pattern that can be used to access a website. For example, wikipedia.org.

user A person that uses a technological device to access a software product.

Vanilla JS When a developer uses pure JavaScript without any framework.

variable While writing code, a variable is a small "box" where you can store values. Values can be a text (known as string), a number (integer or float), a list, and many other types.

war room A room (virtual or physical) where people can join to work together on an incident.

Waterfall methodology A linear approach to developing software, where each step depends on the result of the previous step.

web page A document file that has specific instructions on how it should be presented by a browser.

website A group of web pages, usually in a similar context.

Y career When a senior developer can choose between staying at the engineering path (becoming a principal) or moving to a management path if they want to grow without being pushed to a single career path.

Acronyms

API Application Programming Interface.

B2B Business to Business.

B2C Business to Consumer.

CD Continuous Development.

CI Continuous Integration.

CSS Cascading Style Sheets.

DNS Domain Name System.

HTML Hypertext Markup Language.

HTTP Hypertext Transfer Protocol.

HTTPS Hypertext Transfer Protocol Secure.

IOT Internet of Things.

JS JavaScript.

JSON JavaScript Object Notation.

MVP Minimum Viable Product.

OS Operating System.

PM Confusingly, it can mean project manager or product manager, depending on the organization.

SLA Service Level Agreement.

SPA Single-Page Application.

SQL Structured Query Language.

TDD Test-Driven Development.

TPM Technical Program Manager.

UI User Interface.

URL Uniform Resource Locator.

UX User Experience.

WIP Work in Progress.

XML Extensible Markup Language.

© Leticia Portella 2023
L. Portella, *A Friendly Guide to Software Development*,
https://doi.org/10.1007/978-1-4842-8969-3

Index

A

Agile Manifesto, 143, 144
Agile methodologies, 145, 148, 235, 236, 240
Agile philosophy, 144, 145, 153, 155
Algorithms, 43, 44
Amplify learning, 154
Android, 32, 88
AngularJS, 84
Application Programming Interface (APIs)
    concept, 98–101
    internet, 111
    API, 99
Application software, 33, 34, 40
Asynchronous communication, 242
Authentication, 23, 95
Automated rollback, 212

B

Backend and frontend technologies, 70, 73, 80, 93, 111, 112
Bad code, 172, 189, 221, 222
Bankrupt, 220, 222–223
Big data, 137

Blogs, 68
Bootcamp, 248
Brand-new technology, 138
Broken windows theory, 221
Bugs, 44, 46, 122, 130, 152, 186, 207, 225, 230, 274
Bus factor, 241
Businesses, 115, 229, 271
Business idea, 17
Business logic, 84, 91, 93, 96, 174, 221
Business specialists, 271–272
Business to Business (B2B), 9
Business to Consumer (B2C), 9

C

Cascading Style Sheets (CSS), 78–81, 83, 86, 88, 91
Chaos Monkey, 210
Chaotic environments, 242
Clients, 54, 57, 70, 86–88, 98, 132, 204–207, 224
    dumb, 86, 87
    intelligent, 88, 111
    parisian, 205
Clock masters, 187

© Leticia Portella 2023
L. Portella, *A Friendly Guide to Software Development*,
https://doi.org/10.1007/978-1-4842-8969-3